QUICK QUILTS FOR THE
HOLIDAYS

11 PROJECTS TO STAMP, STENCIL, AND SEW

TRICE BOERENS

C&T PUBLISHING

VWM

© 2002, Trice Boerens
Editor: Pamela Mostek
Technical Editor: Pamela Mostek
Copyeditor/Proofreader: Carol Barrett
Cover Designer: Kristen Yenche
Book Designer: Rohani Design
Design Director: Diane Pedersen
Illustrator: Katherine Petersen
Production Assistant: Kristy A. Konitzer
Photography: Garry Gay unless otherwise noted
Photo styling: Diane Pedersen and Garry Gay
How-to photography: Kevin Dilley
Author photograph: Jeanette Williams
Published by C&T Publishing, Inc., P.O. Box 1456, Lafayette, California 94549

Front cover: Snowman Wallhanging
Back cover: Green Witches and Merry Merry

Attention Teachers: C&T Publishing, Inc. encourages you to use this book as a text for teaching. Contact us at 800-284-1114 or www.ctpub.com for more information about the C&T Teachers Program.

Library of Congress Cataloging-in-Publication Data

Boerens, Trice.
Quick quilts for the holidays : 11 projects to stamp, stencil, and sew / Trice Liljenquist Boerens.
    p. cm.
   ISBN 1-57120-143-2
   1. Quilting—Patterns. 2. Textile painting. 3. Holiday decorations. I. Title.
TT835 .B5135 2002
746.46'041—dc21

2001006674

Printed in China

10 9 8 7 6 5 4 3 2 1

Acknowledgments

❧

Thanks to the staff at C&T Publishing for their vision and for their patience. We all had the same goal, but I took the long way around to reach it.

Thanks to Pam Mostek, my editor, for being right-brained while I was being left-brained.

Thanks to Paula Murray for her inventive machine quilting and her comforting demeanor.

And thanks to my children, Andrew, Cole, Mary, and Allison, for eating a lot of take-out food. I would like to give the impression that they ate a lot of take-out food because I was very busy writing a book . . . but the truth is they have been doing it all their lives.

Contents

Introduction

I grew up with four sisters, and every spring my mother made five Easter dresses. She also made back-to-school clothes, drapes, pillows, dust ruffles, Christmas stockings, and baby quilts; but the best scraps always came from the Easter dresses.

Those scraps were especially inspirational, and I made some crazy quilts with them. I don't mean Crazy Quilts, I mean CRAZY quilts. Little did I know back then, it was just the beginning of many years of creating.

Today when I go into an art supply store, a quilt store, a needlework store, or even the local home improvement center, I get that same old feeling that I did playing with those treasured scraps. Looking around at all the products and supplies, my heart beats a little faster, and I just can't wait to get my hands on some of them. I get that old have-to-make-something feeling! So many paints, fabrics, and copper tubing . . . so little time!

I haven't been able to play with them all . . . but I've given it a good try! In this book I've included some of my favorites like stamping, stenciling, and fabric painting and combined them with simple quilting to make a collection of very fun projects I know you're going to enjoy making.

There are many terrific quilting books on the market today, but I wanted to write my book with just a little different approach. Not just well-designed and easy-to-complete projects . . . but quilts with a touch of art and fancy. My goal was to include simple techniques to add to your quilts that would make them really unique and fun to use.

What better time than the holidays for making a project you can stamp, stencil, and sew. I've included fun quilts for the fall holidays of Halloween and Thanksgiving and lots of great ideas for the winter holidays of Christmas and Hanukkah. And all of them, of course, have those special creative touches that I love!

So whether you're a long-time fan of trying new creative techniques, like I am, or a first-timer, I hope you'll give it a try and add some of these fun ideas to your quilts. Take it from me, there's nothing like jumping right in with something new and creative to get your heart beating just a little faster!

Enjoy yourself!

Trice

Special Techniques

T he special touches of stamping, stenciling, and painting on your quilt will make it fun, fanciful, and uniquely your own! Before you begin, read through the instructions first, and then go back and follow each step. Any special materials, such as stamps, paints, erasers, and other tools, will be included in the Materials list for each project.

STAMPING

Stamping on fabric can be done with purchased stamps or a stamp hand carved from an art gum eraser with a craft knife. I have used both types in the book projects. The Materials list will show you which method I have used, but you can experiment and purchase or make your own for any of the projects. Just follow these simple instructions. Before you stamp your quilt, however, you should do a little practice-stamping on fabric scraps just to get a feel for the process.

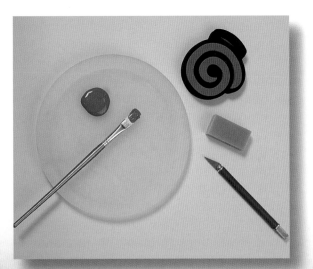

1. Shake the jar of paint before using it. Then use a paintbrush to apply an even coat of paint to the stamp. The consistency is important—thick paint will make an uneven image, and if it's too thin the image will be blurred.

2. Firmly press the stamp in place and remove it without rocking or twisting so that you get a clear image. Blot off extra paint.

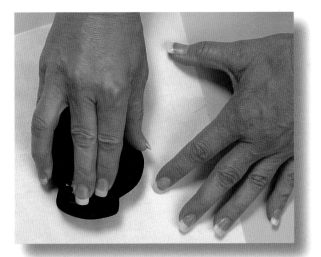

3. Clean the stamp between each stamping with soap, water, and a soft cloth, then allow it to dry thoroughly before using it again.

STENCILING

Stenciling is a great way to easily add a repeated design to your quilt. Template plastic from the quilt shop or Mylar from the craft store both work well as stencil material. You will also need a sharp craft knife for cutting and a fine-tipped permanent marker for tracing, plus a round stencil brush for applying the paint.

1. Trace the pattern onto template plastic or Mylar with a marking pen. You will need to trace a separate stencil for each color you plan to use. With the craft knife, cut out the inside of each traced stencil, leaving at least 3" around all edges before you trace another stencil pattern on the sheet. After you have traced several patterns onto the sheet of plastic, cut it apart so that each stencil is on a separate portion of the sheet. This way you won't have a larger sheet of plastic overlapping wet stencil paint as you work.

2. Place the stencil on the fabric and hold securely or tape it in place. With a stencil brush, apply the paint with short up and down strokes which is called *pouncing*. Let it dry between applications.

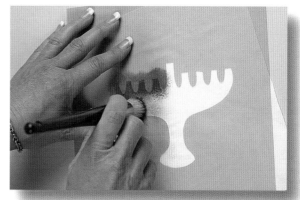

3. When the paint is completely dry, carefully remove the stencil. Refer to the manufacturer's instructions for heat setting the paint.

PAINTING

You can paint on your quilt with fabric paints or with acrylic craft paints with a textile medium such as Acclaim Fabri-Tex added. Your local craft store will have an assortment for you to choose from. Just follow the manufacturer's instructions for details on clean up or use. A fine-tipped brush is great for adding details and a larger brush for applying background washes.

To create a *feathered* edge on a painted area, first add water to the fabric with a brush until it is damp, then dilute the paint with water so that it has a transparent quality when it is applied. As it dries, it will leave a feathered edge. Experiment on scraps of fabric before trying this technique on your project—in order to create this pleasing effect, it is necessary to add just the right amount of water.

Autumn Holidays

You can almost feel it in the air . . .
golden autumn has arrived. The days
of hot summer sun and bright, bloom-
ing gardens are behind us, and it's time to celebrate
the season of bountiful garden harvests and crisp,
falling leaves. You will be ready to welcome these
autumn holidays when you create wonderful
stamped and stenciled projects to add to your
autumn décor.

Green Witches

It wouldn't be Halloween without witches . . . especially green witches! Welcome the spooky season with this easy-to-make wallhanging with fun finishing touches of stamping and stenciling.

MATERIALS

Finished size: 21¾" x 29½"

Black fabric – ⅓ yard
Green fabric – ½ yard
Gray fabric – ⅓ yard
Light green, yellow fabric – scraps or
    small pieces
Backing – ¾ yard
Binding – ⅓ yard
Batting – 26" x 33½" piece
Fusible web – scrap or small piece
Embroidery floss – black
Template plastic or Mylar
Black fabric marker
Star stamp – approximately 1⅞"-wide
Spiral stamp – approximately 1½" in
    diameter
Fabric or craft paint – yellow, purple,
    cream, gray
Stencil brush

Cutting

Black
Cut one 2"-wide strip, then cut into
    Two 18¼" pieces
Cut one 6"-wide strip, then cut into
    Four 7¼" pieces
Green
Cut one 5"-wide strip, then cut into
    Four 4½" pieces
    Two 5¼" pieces
    Four 3" pieces
Cut one 3¾"-wide strip, then cut into
    Two 7¼" pieces
Cut one 2¼"-wide strip, then cut into
    Four 7¼" pieces
Gray
Cut four 2½"-wide strips, then cut into
    Two 22¼" strips
    Two 26" strips
Binding
Cut four 2½" x 42" strips

Assembly

1. Trace the face pattern on page 14 onto template plastic and cut out. Trace around the template four times onto light green fabric.

2. Refer to "Stenciling" on page 9. Cut the face stencil, and with cream paint stencil on the left side of each traced face. Let dry and cut out, leaving ¼" seam allowance around each.

3. Trace the hat pattern from page 17 onto template plastic and cut out. Trace around the template four times onto black fabric. Cut out leaving ¼" seam allowance around all edges.

4. Refer to "Hand Appliqué" on page 86 and stitch the hats and faces onto four 4½" x 5" green pieces.

Make four

5. Sew two 3" x 5" green pieces, one 5" x 5¼" piece, and two face units together as shown to make a strip. Sew a 2" x 18¼" black sleeve strip to the bottom. Repeat to make two face strips.

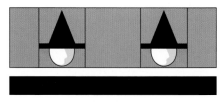

Make two

6. Sew together two 2¼" x 7¼" green pieces, one 3¾" x 7¼" green piece, and two 6" x 7¼" black pieces as shown to make the skirt row. Repeat to make two rows.

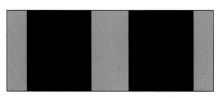

Make two

7. Sew two face strips and two skirt strips together as shown. Press. Sew the 2½" x 26" border strips to the sides and the 2½" x 22¼" border strips to the top and bottom. Press.

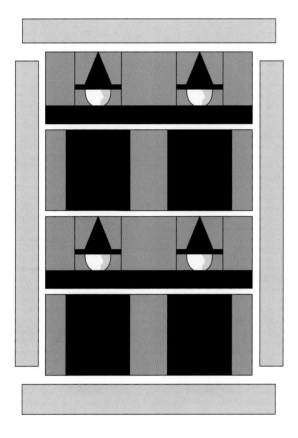

Finishing

1. Refer to "Fusible Appliqué" on page 87. On the paper side of the fusible web, trace five stars from the pattern on page 17. Iron them onto yellow fabric and trim. Position on the wallhanging and fuse in place.

2. Blanket stitch around each star with one strand of embroidery floss, referring to "Embroidery Stitches" on page 92.

3. Trace the cat pattern onto template plastic and cut out. Referring to "Stenciling" on page 9, use gray paint to stencil the cat on the dress of the lower right witch. Let dry.

4. With black fabric marker draw the witch and cat faces. Heat set marker.

5. Refer to "Stamping" on page 8. With the yellow paint and spiral stamp, stamp spirals on the hats. With purple paint and the spiral and star stamps, randomly stamp spirals and stars on the dresses. Let dry.

6. Referring to "Layering and Quilting" on page 90, layer the wallhanging top, batting, and backing together and baste. Quilt as desired.

7. Refer to "Binding" on page 90 and sew the binding to the wallhanging.

Quick Quilts for the Holidays

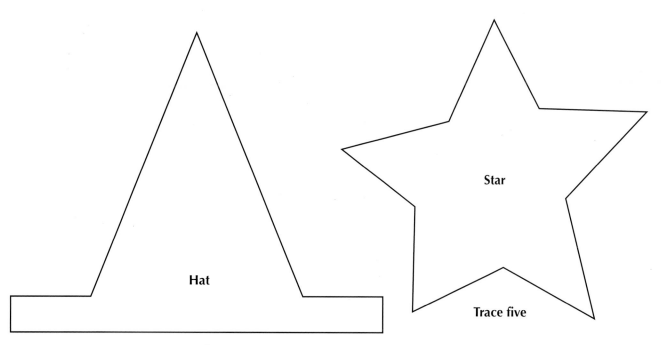

Hat

Trace four

Star

Trace five

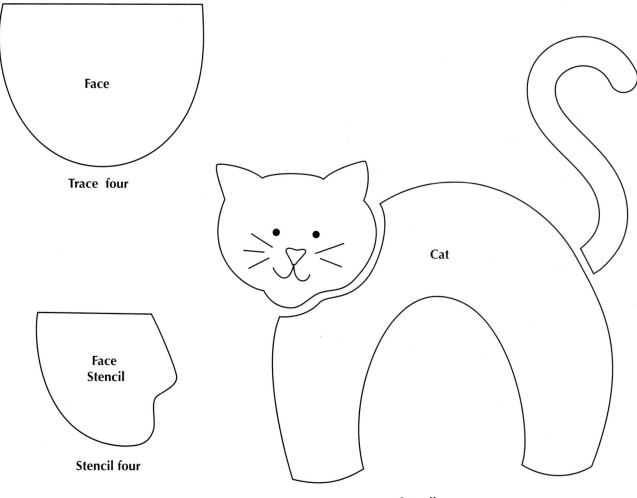

Face

Trace four

Face
Stencil

Stencil four

Cat

Stencil one

Pumpkin Nights

From his spot on the garden fence, this pumpkin keeps a watchful eye on the Halloween skies . . . just in case witches and goblins fly by. Stamping and hand appliqué make this wallhanging truly a ghostly delight!

MATERIALS

Finished size: 18¾" x 23"

Black fabric – ¾ yard (including binding)

White fabric – ⅛ yard

Turquoise fabric – ⅓ yard

Dark print fabric – 5½" x 12" piece

Orange fabric – 8" x 8" piece

Green fabric – scraps for appliqué

Backing – ¾ yard

Batting – 23" x 28" piece

Template plastic or Mylar

Black fabric marker

Star stamp – approximately 1⅞"-wide

Paintbrush

Fabric or craft paint – cream, light gray

Three black buttons – about ½" diameter

Cutting

Black

Cut one 14¾" x 16" piece

Cut one 1¼"-wide strip, then cut into
    Nine 3½" pieces

Cut three 2½" x 42" strips for binding

White

Cut two 1¼"-wide strips, then cut into
    Ten 3½" pieces
    One 14¾" piece

Turquoise

Cut three 2¾"-wide strips, then cut into
    Two 14¾" strips
    Two 23¾" strips

Dark print fabric

Cut two 5" squares

Assembly

1. Beginning with a white strip, sew together the ten white 1¼" x 3½" strips and the nine black 1¼" x 3½" strips to make one fence unit that is 14¾" x 3½". It may be necessary to take in or let out a few seams so that the fence unit measures 14¾".

2. Cut the fence unit in half lengthwise to make two 14¾" x 1¾" strips. Sew the 14¾" white strip between the two pieced fence strips. Press toward center strip.

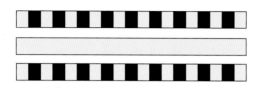

3. With right sides together, sew the fence to the shorter side of the 14¾" x 16" black piece. Press.

4. Sew the two shorter turquoise border strips to the top and bottom. Press. Sew the longer turquoise border strips to the sides and press.

5. On the two 5" dark print squares, draw a diagonal line on the wrong side of the fabric from corner to corner. With right sides together position one square on each top border corner as shown and stitch on the drawn line. Trim to ¼" seam allowance and press.

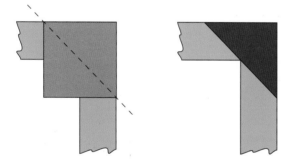

Finishing

1. Trace the pumpkin and stem patterns from page 21 onto template plastic and cut out. Adding a ³⁄₁₆"–¼" turn-under allowance to each piece, trace around the pumpkin onto orange fabric and the stem onto green fabric. Cut out and appliqué in place referring to "Hand Appliqué" on page 86.

2. Refer to "Stamping" on page 8. With the star stamp and cream paint, stamp seven stars in the sky.

3. With the black fabric marker, draw the eye circles and nose on the pumpkin. Paint crescents for whites of eyes with light grey paint. Sew on buttons for the eye centers and mouth.

4. Referring to "Layering and Quilting" on page 90, layer the wallhanging top, batting, and backing together and baste. Quilt as desired.

5. Refer to "Binding" on page 90 to add binding to the wallhanging.

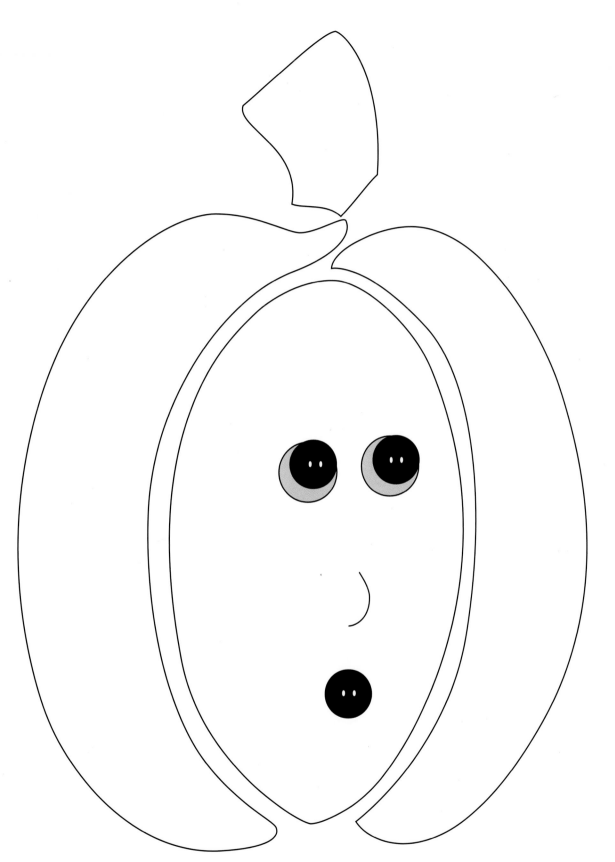

Cut one of each

Bountiful Harvest

Celebrate autumn's abundant garden harvest and add this unique table runner to your Thanksgiving table. Pieced vegetables are accented with a message of "Give Thanks" for this bountiful season.

MATERIALS

Finished size: 11½" x 44¼"

Red fabric – ⅜ yard
Green fabric – ¼ yard
Cream fabric – ¼ yard
Orange fabric – ¼ yard
Cream print fabric – ⅛ yard
Purple fabric – ⅛ yard
Green plaid fabric – ⅛ yard
Dark red fabric – ⅛ yard
Backing – 1 yard
Batting – 16" x 51½" piece
Embroidery floss – cream
Air soluble marker
Black fabric marker

Cutting

Red
Cut one 12" x 25" piece

Green
Cut one 1"-wide strip, then cut into
    One 12" piece
    Ten 1" squares

Cut three 1½"-wide strips, then cut into
    Four 1" pieces
    Thirty-six 1½" squares
    Four 2" pieces
    Twelve 2½" pieces
    Four 3" pieces
    Six 3½" pieces

Cream
Cut one ¾"-wide strip, then cut into
    Forty ¾" squares
Cut one 1¾"-wide strip, then cut into
    Two 12" pieces
Cut one 1½"-wide strip, then cut into
    Eight 2" pieces

Orange
Cut one 1" x 18" piece
Cut two 1½"-wide strips, then cut into
    Thirty 1½" squares

Cream print
Cut one 1¼"-wide strip, then cut into
    Two 12" pieces

Purple
Cut one 1¼"-wide strip, then cut into
    Two 12" pieces

Green plaid
Cut two 1"-wide strips, then cut into
    Ten 1½" pieces
    One 12" piece
    One 18" piece

Dark red
Cut one 2"-wide strip, then cut into
    Ten 2" squares

Assembly

1. To make the AB units, position ten 1" green squares on the end of ten 1" x 1½" green plaid pieces with right sides together. Sew them diagonally from corner to corner as shown. Trim seam allowance to ¼" and press.

Make ten

2. To make the CD units, stitch one 1" x 12" green plaid piece to one 1" x 12" green piece to make a strip set. Cut the strip set into ten 1" segments.

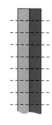

Cut ten segments

3. To make the EF units, repeat step 2 using one 1" x 18" green plaid piece and one 1" x 18" orange piece. Cut into ten 1½" segments.

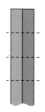

Cut ten segments

4. To make the GH units, position twenty green 1½" squares and twenty orange 1½" squares with right sides together. Stitch diagonally from corner to corner, trim the seam allowance to ¼" and press.

Make twenty

5. Using units AB, CD, EF, GH, green background pieces, and orange squares, assemble two end sections in rows 1-11 according to the layout diagram. Sew the rows together using a scant ¼" seam allowance. It may be necessary to take in or let out seams so that the border section measures 12". Trim the side and top rectangle pieces so that they are even with the adjoining pieces as shown.

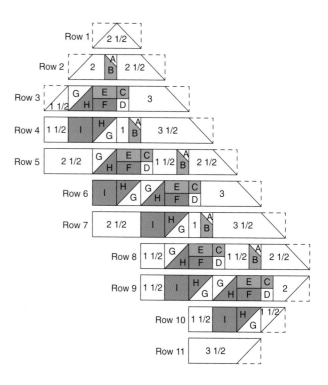

6. With right sides together, position a ¾" cream square on the corners of a 2" dark red square. Stitch diagonally from corner to corner, trim the seam allowance to ¼" and press. Repeat to make ten beets.

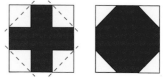

7. Sew the 2" x 1½" cream pieces between the beets as shown to make two border strips. Take in or let out the seams slightly if necessary so that the strip measures 12" wide. Sew the cream strip to the top and the purple strip to the bottom. Press.

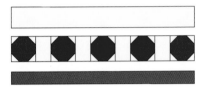

8. Assemble the pieced carrot units, pieced beet units, and cream print strips to make two end units. Sew the 12" x 25" center red piece between them. Press.

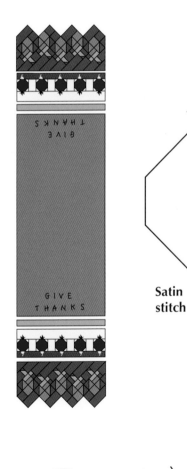

Finishing

1. With three strands of cream embroidery floss, satin stitch bottoms on the beets, referring to "Embroidery Stitches" on page 92. Add the tops with a fabric marker and heat set.

2. Using the lettering guide below, write "Give Thanks" on each end of the table runner with an air soluble marker. Go over the letters with a fabric marker and heat set.

3. Cut two 16" x 26" backing pieces and sew the short sides together. Position the table runner top and backing with right sides together on top of batting. Using the edge of the table runner as a guide, machine stitch through all the layers ¼" from the edge. Leave a 6" opening on the side for turning. Trim the backing and batting even with the wallhanging top.

4. Trim the ends of the border points and clip the inside corners to the stitching line. Turn right side out, press, and hand stitch the opening.

Trim ends

Clip corners

5. Machine quilt in the seam lines of the border strips and in the center as desired.

Satin stitch

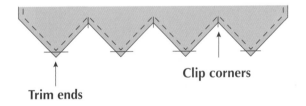

Autumn Wreath

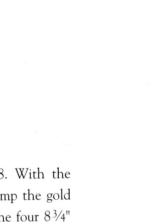

Greet your Thanksgiving guests with this harvest wreath of apples, pears, and other abundant fruits of the season. You'll create it using hand appliqué, stamping, and stenciling . . . and for a finishing touch, a ribbon bow.

MATERIALS

Finished size: 25¼" square

Gold fabric – ⅓ yard
Green fabric – ⅓ yard
Tan fabric – ½ yard
Olive green fabric – ¼ yard
Dark green, Christmas green, purple, lavender, red, orange, pink print, and yellow print fabrics – scraps or small pieces for appliqué
Backing – ⅞ yard
Batting – 30" square piece
Fabric or craft paint – purple, violet, tan, dark brown
Paisley stamp – approximately 2" x 4"
Paintbrush
Embroidery floss – brown, rust, olive green, purple
Art gum eraser
Craft knife
Freezer paper
Air soluble marker
Wired ribbon – 2" x 36" (optional)

Cutting

Gold
Cut one 8¾"-wide strip, then cut into
    Four 8¾" squares
Green
Cut one 1¼"-wide strip, then cut into
    Two 8¾" pieces
    One 17¾" piece
Cut four 2"-wide strips
Tan
Cut four 3"-wide strips

Assembly

1. Refer to "Stamping" on page 8. With the paisley stamp and tan paint, stamp the gold fabric in a random pattern on the four 8¾" squares of gold fabric. Let dry.

2. Dilute the dark brown paint with water so that it is transparent. Experiment on stamped

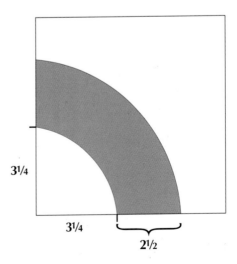

3¼

3¼

2½

fabric scraps to make sure you have added enough water. The paint should be transparent enough to reveal the paisley print beneath the paint. With the diluted paint, paint arcs on each square as shown. Let dry.

3. To make the stamp for grapes, draw a ½" diameter circle on the end of an art gum eraser. With a craft knife score and cut away the background around the circle to approximately ⅛" deep.

Cut away background

4. With the purple and violet paints, stamp grapes on the four gold fabric squares as shown, overlapping some of the grapes. Let dry.

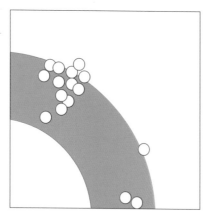

Make three

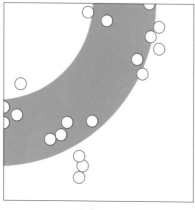

Make one

5. Referring to "Hand Appliqué" on page 86, trace the appliqué shapes from pages 29 and 30 onto freezer paper and cut out. Iron them onto selected fabrics and trim, leaving a ³⁄₁₆"–¼" turn-under allowance around each. Position, pin, and stitch the appliqués onto four gold squares. You will be making three of Block A and one of Block B.

6. Sew a 1¼" x 8¾" green strip between one Block A and Block B to make the right section of the wreath. Sew a 1¼" x 8¾" green strip between two remaining Block A's to make the left wreath section. Press. Sew the 1¼" x 17¾" green strip between the wreath sections as shown.

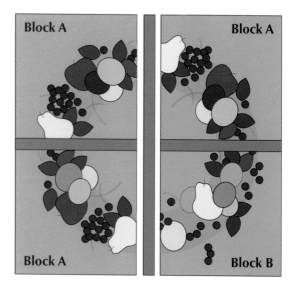

7. Refer to "Mitered Borders" on page 87 and add mitered borders to the quilt.

8. Using the freezer-paper technique, make an olive green fabric bow from the pattern on page 31 and add embroidery details. Appliqué it to the wallhanging, or add a ribbon bow.

9. Draw the stems and twigs onto the wreath with an air soluble marker. Refer to "Embroidery Stitches" on page 92 and satin stitch the twigs using rust embroidery floss. Using brown embroidery floss, backstitch the stems. Stitch dimples on plums with purple.

Block A
Make three

Finishing

1. Position the wallhanging and backing with right sides together and place on top of the batting. Stitch around the outside edge with a ¼" seam allowance, leaving a 6" opening on the side for turning. Trim the backing and batting edge even with the wallhanging top.

2. Turn with right sides out, press, and hand stitch the opening closed. Machine quilt in the seam lines of the wreath and border. Add a ribbon bow on top of the appliqué bow if desired.

Block measures   8¾"

Block B
Make one

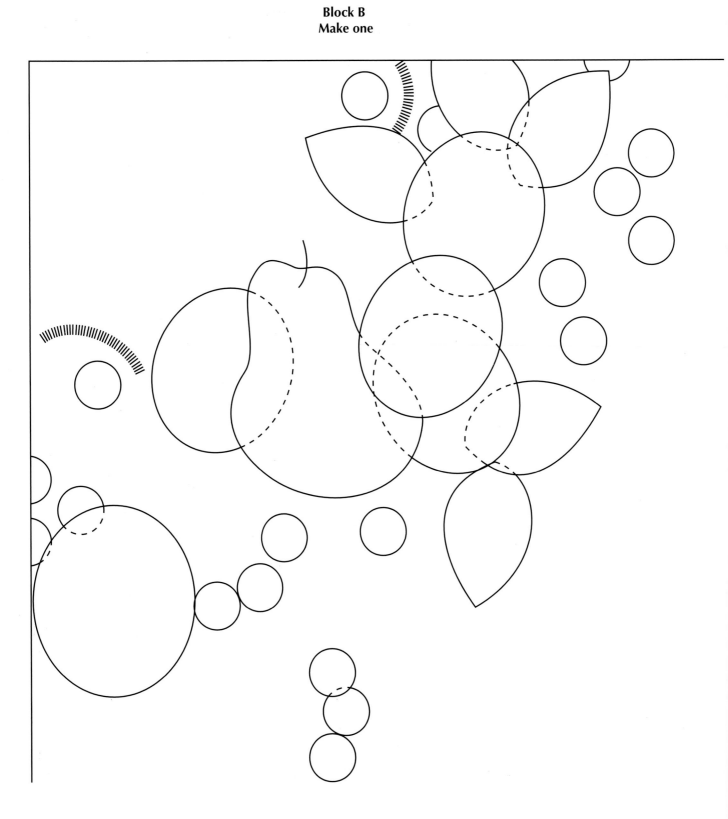

Block measures   8³/₄"

Winter Holidays

I t's everyone's favorite season . . . outside the soft snow is falling, and inside the cozy fire is crackling. There's just a certain magic in the air when winter makes its annual arrival. And what could be more magical than the wonderful winter holidays with Santas, snowmen, and other delights. You'll add your own magic touch to your holiday home with these festive projects to stamp and stencil with holiday cheer!

Snowman Wallhanging

What better way to greet the winter season than with this happy holiday snowman. He is joined by festive Christmas stockings and stars, and tasty treats galore. Fusible appliqué, stamping, and stenciling add the fanciful finishing touches.

MATERIALS

Finished size: 22" x 30½"

Blue fabric – ⅓ yard
White fabric – ¼ yard
Assorted cream print fabrics – ½ yard total
Assorted turquoise print fabrics – ¼ yard total
Pink print – ⅛ yard
Violet, purple, tan, green, yellow, peach, pink, black – scraps or small pieces for appliques
Backing – ¾ yard
Binding – ⅓ yard
Batting – 26" x 36" piece
Fusible web – ¼ yard
Black fabric marker
Template plastic or Mylar
Spiral stamp – approximately 1⅞" in diameter
Paintbrush
Stencil brush
Craft knife

Fabric or craft paint – pink, purple, light blue, orange
Small white beads – approximately 20–25
Pink buttons – three, about 9/16" in diameter

Cutting

Blue
Cut one 3¼" x 5¼" piece
 One 5" x 3¼" piece
 Two 3" x 5¾" pieces
 One 6" square
 One 4½" x 4¾" piece
 Two 4" x 3¾" pieces
 Two 1¼" squares
 Four 1½" squares
 Two 1¾" squares
 One 4¼" x 12½" piece

White
Cut one 3¼" square
 One 6" square
 One 3¾" x 5½" piece
 One 5¾" x 7½" piece
 One 1½" x 14" piece

Assorted cream prints
Cut one 5¼" x 18¾" piece
 Four 2¼" x 4½" pieces and four 2½" squares from the same fabric
 One 7" x 17¼" piece
 Three 4¼" x 4¾" pieces

Assorted turquoise prints

Cut one 5¾" x 11¾" piece
  One 5¼" x 12½" piece
  One 1½" x 14" piece

Pink print

Cut two 1½" x 4¾" pieces
  One 1¾" x 15½" piece

Violet

Cut one 1½" x 5¼" piece

Binding

Cut four 2½" x 42"-wide strips

Assembly

1. Position two 1¼" blue squares on the top two corners of the 3¼" white square. Stitch diagonally from corner to corner on the blue squares and trim seam allowance to ¼". Press.

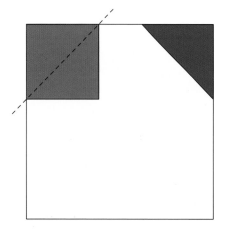

2. Sew the snowman head from step 1 between 3¼" x 5¼" and 3¼" x 5" blue background pieces. Press.

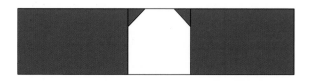

3. Repeat step 1 to sew two 1½" blue squares on the corners of a 5½" x 3¾" white piece. Repeat step 2 to sew body between two 3¾" x 4" blue pieces.

4. Repeat step 1 to sew two 1½" blue squares on the top corners and two 1¾" blue squares on the bottom corners of a 5¾" x 7½" white piece. Sew the snowman base between two 3" x 5¾" blue pieces.

5. Sew together the 4¼" x 12½" blue piece and the snowman sections. Press.

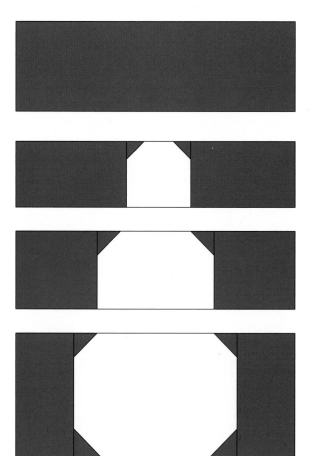

6. Sew two 1½" x 4¾" pink pieces between three 4¼" x 4¾" cream pieces. Press.

7. Sew the 1½" x 5¼" violet piece on the end of the 5¼" x 18¾" cream print piece. Press.

8. Sew together the pieced sections and the 1¾" x 15½" pink strip as shown.

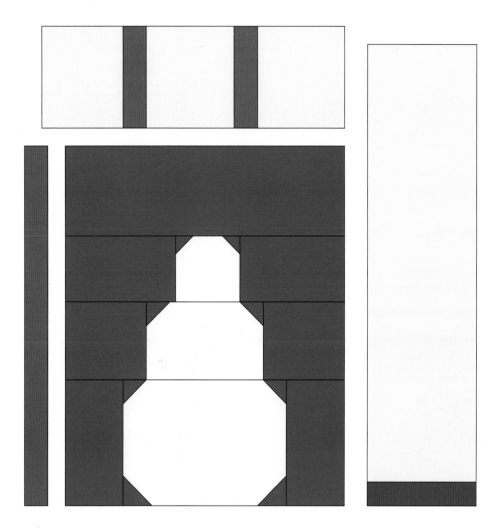

9. Sew the 1½" x 14" white strip and the 1½" x 14" turquoise strip together lengthwise. Press. Cut into eight 1½" segments.

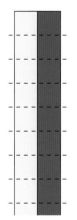

10. Sew two segments together to make four Four-Patch blocks. Press.

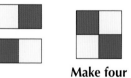

Make four

11. Sew together a Four-Patch block, a 2¼" x 4½" cream piece, and a 2½" cream square. Press. Repeat to make four.

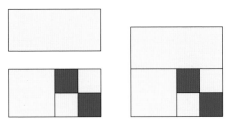

Make four

12. Sew units from step 11 together in a vertical row and sew the 4½" x 4¾" blue piece to the top.

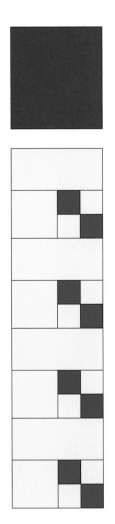

13. Cut a 6" blue square and 6" white square in half diagonally twice. Sew a blue and white triangle together as shown. Repeat to make two. Save the extra triangles for another project.

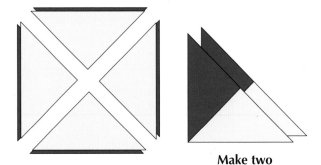

Make two

14. Sew triangle units from step 13 together as shown to make one triangle square. Press.

15. Sew the triangle square, the 5¼" x 12½" turquoise print piece, the 7" x 17¼" cream print piece, and the 5¾" x 11¾" turquoise print piece together. Assemble as shown.

Finishing

1. Refer to "Fusible Appliqué" on page 87. Trace patterns for the hat, feather, twig arms, cupcake tops and bottoms, lollipop circles and stems, wrapped candies, trees and trunks, stockings and cuffs, and stars onto fusible web.

2. Fuse onto the fabrics. Cut out, position, and fuse to the quilt top.

3. Machine stitch around the edges of the fused appliqués.

4. Refer to "Stamping" on page 8. With pink paint and spiral stamp, add the design to lollipops. Let dry.

5. With black fabric marker draw eyes, mouth, and spiral buttons on the snowman. Heat set the marker. Add the nose and glow lines around stars with orange paint and let dry.

6. From the patterns on pages 42 and 43, cut stencils for the wrapped candy design, toes, and heels, referring to "Stenciling" on page 9. With light blue paint, stencil toes and heels on stockings. Let dry. With purple paint stencil design on the wrapped candy. Let dry.

7. Hand stitch small white beads to the hat and trees in a random pattern. Hand stitch buttons to the cupcakes.

8. Cut a 26" x 36" piece from the backing fabric. Refer to "Layering and Quilting" on page 90 and layer the top, batting, and backing. Quilt as desired.

9. Refer to "Binding" on page 90 and sew binding to the wall hanging.

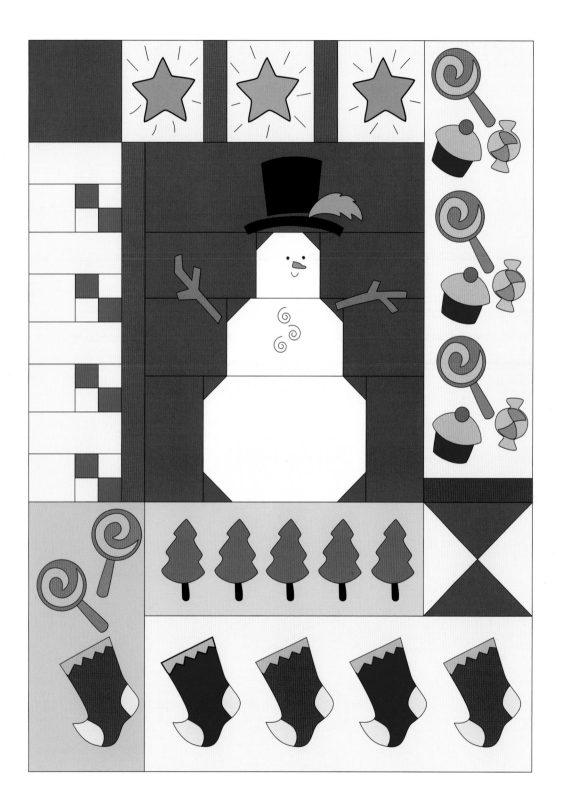

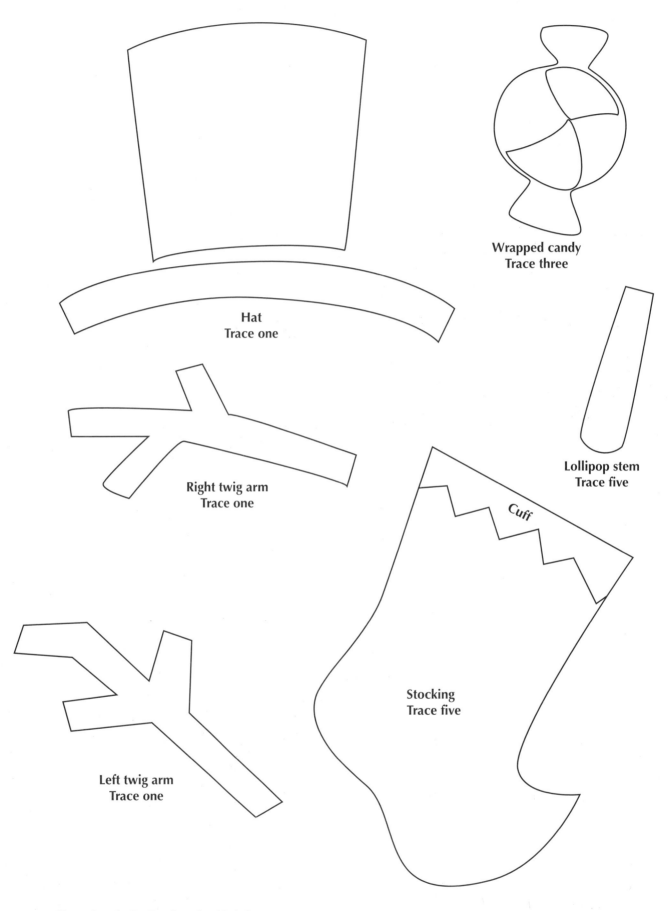

Wrapped candy
Trace three

Hat
Trace one

Lollipop stem
Trace five

Right twig arm
Trace one

Cuff

Stocking
Trace five

Left twig arm
Trace one

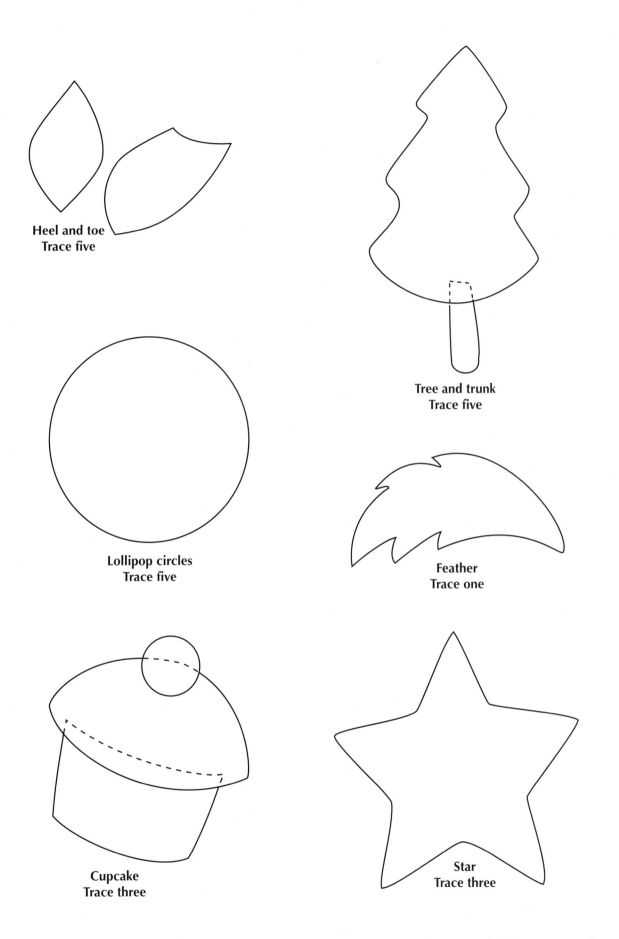

Heel and toe
Trace five

Tree and trunk
Trace five

Lollipop circles
Trace five

Feather
Trace one

Cupcake
Trace three

Star
Trace three

Wreath of Santas

If one Santa is good . . . then six Santas is a celebration! And a celebration is what you will create when you hang this delightful wreath of Santas. You'll make your Santas in no time at all using the quick techniques of fusible appliqué and a fabric marker.

MATERIALS

Finished size: 25" x 39"

Red fabric – ¾ yard
Purple fabric – ⅔ yard
Blue fabric – ⅓ yard
Green fabric – ⅓ yard
Red prints, dark print, cream print –
    scraps or small pieces
Camel-colored felt – ¼ yard (36" wide)
Backing – 1¼ yards
Binding – ½ yard
Batting – 29" x 44" piece
Fusible web – ⅓ yard
Template plastic or Mylar
Red thread
Freezer paper
Black fabric marker
Tan colored pencil
Buttons – approximately 50 of various
    colors and sizes, ⅜"–⅞"-wide

Making the Santas

1. From the patterns on pages 49–51, trace the face, skirt, fur, left coat, right coat, and hat onto template plastic and cut out.

2. Group the fabric scraps together in order to make three Santas in each of two color schemes. Use the cream fabric for all six. Refer to "Fusible Appliqué" on page 87 and trace around each template six times onto fusible web. Fuse to the fabric and cut out.

3. Layer Santa pieces onto camel-colored felt and fuse. With red thread, machine satin stitch around fur pieces and outside edge. Trim felt to ⅛" from the stitching.

4. With black fabric marker draw the faces and beards. With tan colored pencil, lightly color face.

Assembly

1. Trace patterns A, B, C, and D/E from pages 49–51 onto freezer paper and cut them out. Iron three of template A onto green fabric and three onto blue fabric. Iron four of template C onto red fabric. Iron templates B, D, and E onto purple fabric and cut out. Remove freezer paper.

2. Alternating colors, sew six of piece A together to make the wreath, being careful to stop stitching ¼" from the inside edge. Press.

Stop stitching ¼" from
end of seamline

3. Stitching ¼" from the inside edge of the circle and pivoting at each seam, sew piece B to the inside circle of the wreath. Press.

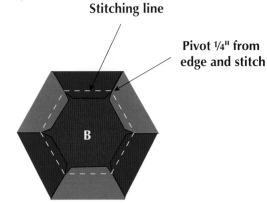

Stitching line

Pivot ¼" from
edge and stitch

B

4. Sew C pieces to the top and bottom of the wreath. Press.

5. Add piece D to the top of the wreath and piece E to the bottom, pivoting and turning at the seam intersections. Cut two 3" x 35" purple strips. Stitch the strips to sides of the banner and press. Trim the bottom ends of the strips to continue the diagonal line of the banner.

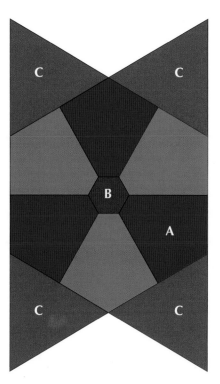

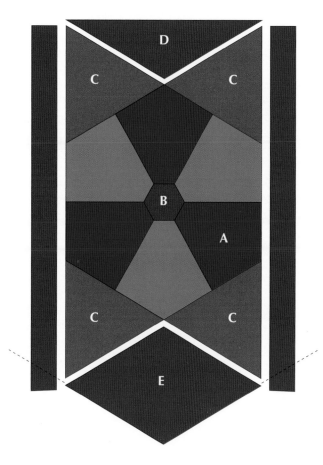

Finishing

1. Cut a 29" x 44" piece from the backing fabric. Referring to "Layering and Quilting" on page 90, layer the banner top, batting, and backing and baste through all layers. Quilt as desired.

2. Refer to "Binding" on page 90. Cut four 2½"-wide binding strips and add binding to the quilt.

3. Pin the Santa appliqués to the A pieces and hand stitch them in place. Sew buttons to the banner between the Santas as shown in the photograph.

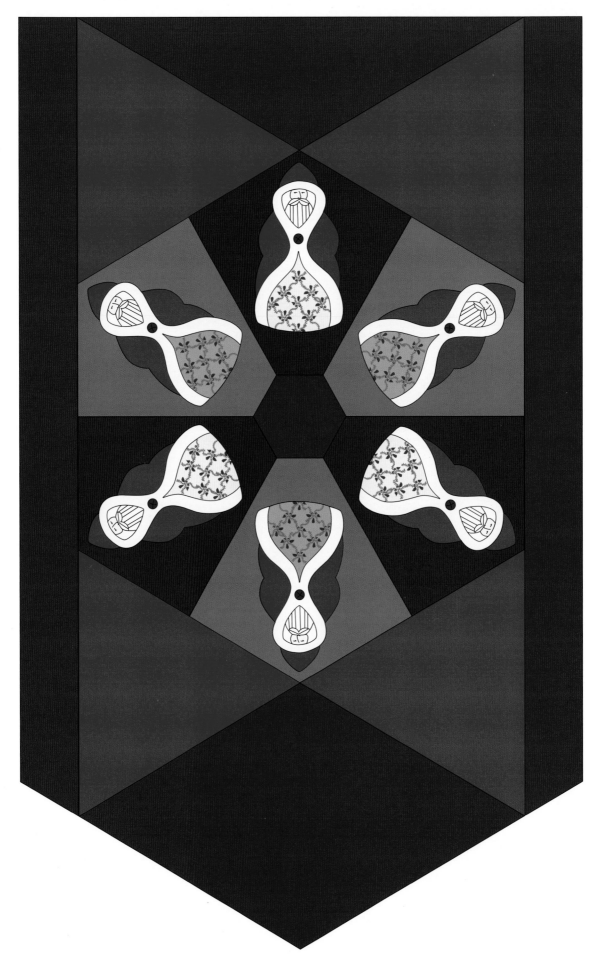

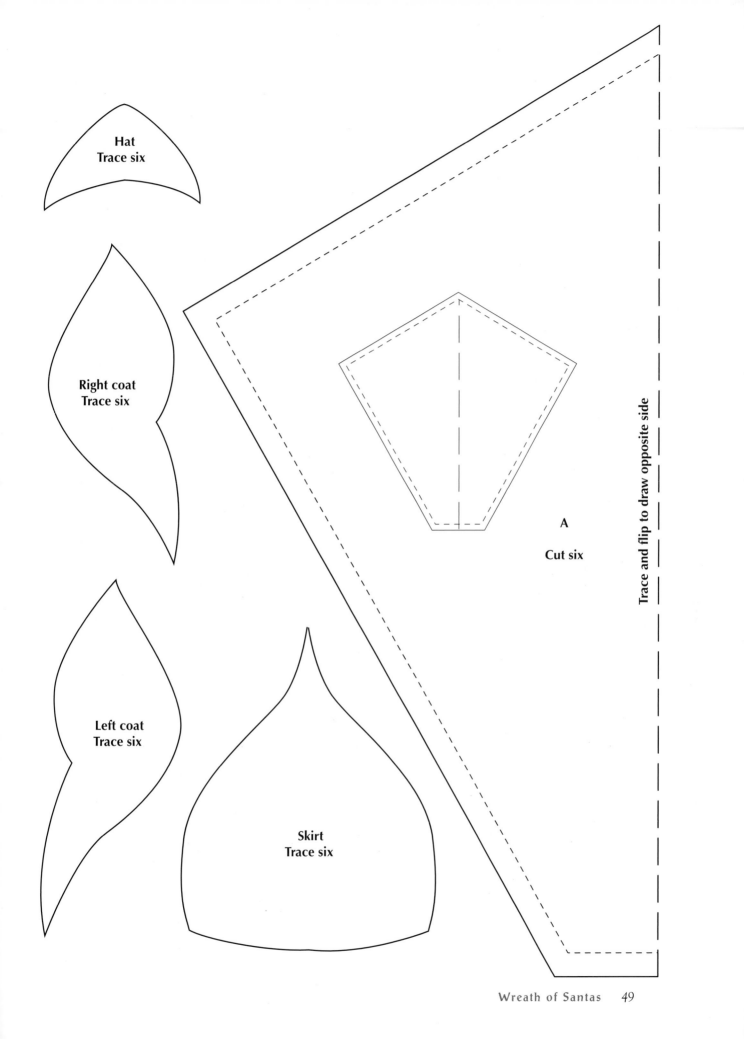

Hat
Trace six

Right coat
Trace six

Left coat
Trace six

Skirt
Trace six

A

Cut six

Trace and flip to draw opposite side

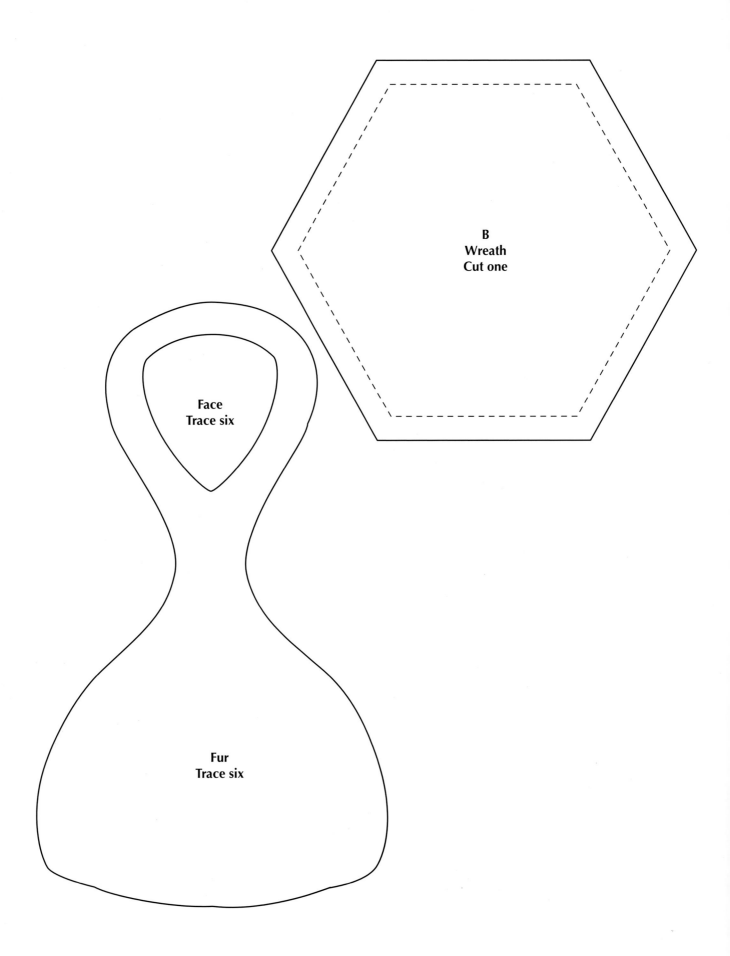

B
Wreath
Cut one

Face
Trace six

Fur
Trace six

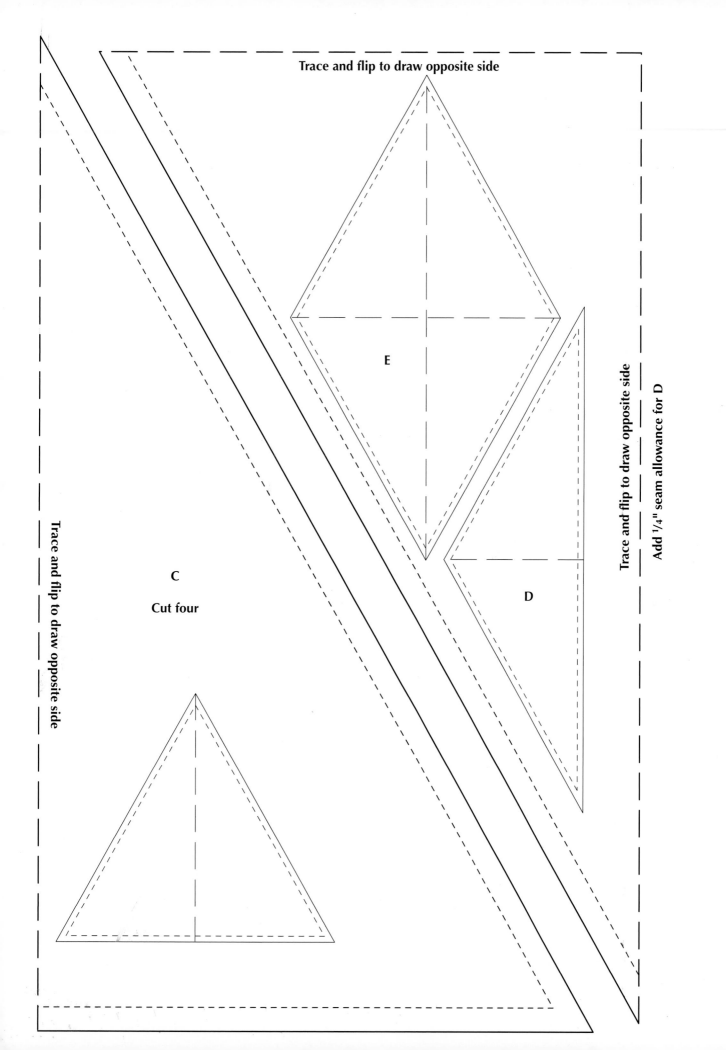

Trace and flip to draw opposite side

E

Trace and flip to draw opposite side

Add ¹/₄" seam allowance for D

C

Cut four

D

Trace and flip to draw opposite side

Peppermint Cats

Peppermint stripes and candies team up with fanciful felines in this quilt of Christmas red and green. You'll have fun stenciling the cats before you appliqué them to this easy-to-piece quilt.

MATERIALS

Finished size: 44½" x 52½"

Assorted green fabrics – 2½ yards total

Striped narrow border – 1¼ yards

Outside border – 1⅝ yards

Backing – 3¼ yards

Binding – ½ yard

Batting – 48" x 57" piece

White fabric for stenciling – ⅓ yard

Red felt – ½ yard (36" wide)

Craft knife

Template plastic or Mylar

Stencil brush

Fabric or craft paint – dark brown, medium brown, green, pink, red

Black fabric marker

Cutting

From the assorted green fabrics, cut:

Section A

One 9½" x 16¼" piece

One 9½" x 10" piece

One 9½" x 9¾" piece

Section B

One 10½" x 10½" square

One 10½" x 11½" piece

One 7½" x 21½" piece

Section C

One 5¾" x 14" piece

One 12¼" x 14" piece

Section D

One 5½" x 9½" piece

One 5½" x 16½" piece

One 5½" x 13½" piece

Section E

One 6½" x 14½" piece

One 6½" x 22½" piece

One 4" x 26½" strip

One 5" x 38½" strip

Binding

Cut five 2½" x 42" strips

Because the background pieces are similar in size and color, take a few minutes to label and organize them as you cut. It will save you time later when you begin to sew. Write the dimensions on a scrap of paper and pin to each fabric piece or write them on masking tape to stick on each one. Use small plastic bags to keep each section separate.

Assembly

1. To make Section A of the quilt center, sew together the 9½" x 16¼" piece, the 9½" x 10" piece, and the 9½" x 9¾" piece. Press.

Section A

2. To make Section B, sew together the 10½" square, the 10½" x 11½" piece, and the 7½" x 21½" piece. Press.

Section B

3. To make Section C, sew together the 5¾" x 14" piece and the 12¼" x 14" piece. Press.

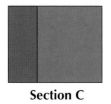

Section C

4. To make Section D, sew the 5½" x 9½" piece, the 5½" x 16½" piece, and the 5½" x 13½" piece together in a vertical strip. Press. To make Section E, sew together the short ends of the 6½" x 14½" piece and the 6½" x 22½" piece. Press.

5. Assemble Sections A, B, C, D, E, the 4" x 26½" green strip, and the 5" x 38½" green strip as shown. Press.

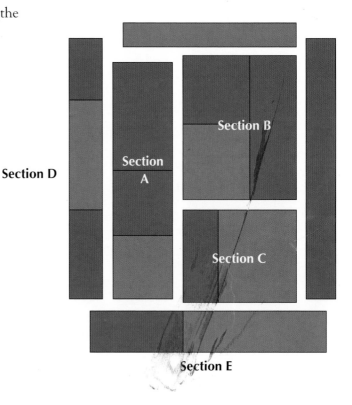

Section D

Section B

Section A

Section C

Section E

6. Refer to "Bias Strips" on page 89 to cut 1¾"-wide bias strips for the inside border. Refer to "Mitered Borders" on page 87 to determine the length you will need for both the inside and outside 3½"-wide border strips. Sew the inside and outside border strips together lengthwise and follow the instructions for mitered borders.

Finishing

1. Trace the circle, candy, leaves, head, stripes, and body patterns from below onto template plastic and cut out. Trace eleven circles onto white fabric leaving at least 1" between each circle. Referring to "Stenciling" on page 9, stencil the cat head and body in the center of each circle and let dry.

2. Stencil the stripes on each cat and let dry. Stencil the candy and leaves and let dry.

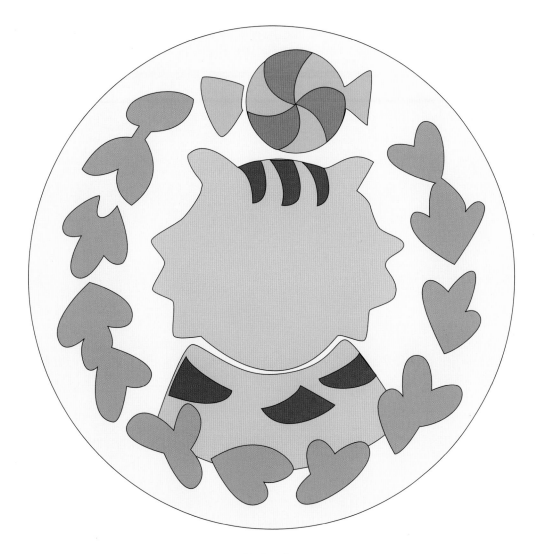

Make eleven

3. With the black fabric marker draw on the face and whiskers. Heat set the marker.

4. Cut out eleven red felt circles adding ⅛" to the circle all around.

5. Cut out the white stenciled circles leaving ³⁄₁₆"–¼" turn-under allowance. Refer to "Hand Appliqué" on page 86 and appliqué the white circles to the red felt circles. Hand stitch the red felt circles to the quilt top as shown in the color photo.

6. Referring to "Layering and Quilting" on page 90, layer the top, batting, and backing together and baste. Quilt as desired.

7. Refer to "Binding" on page 90 and sew binding to quilt.

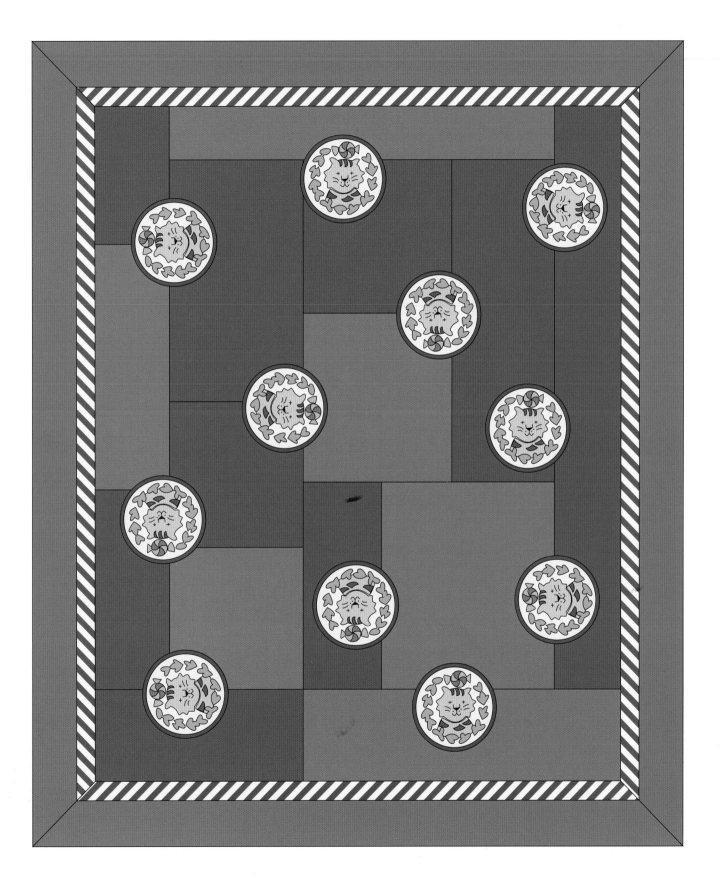

Menorah Table Runner

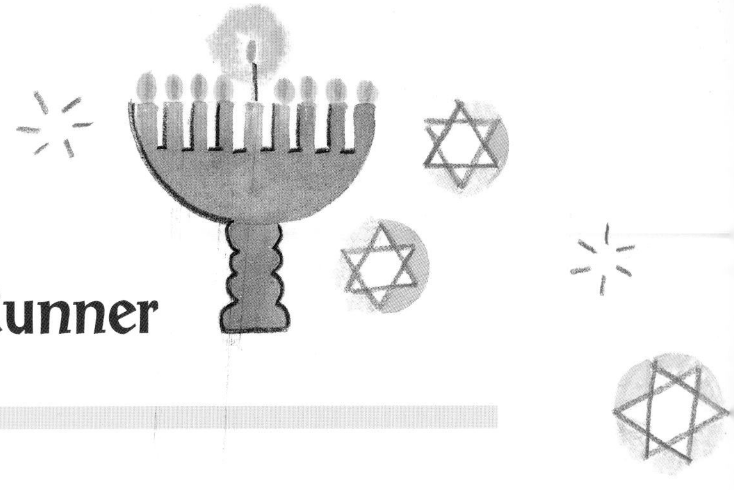

The soft glow of flickering candlelight will add a touch of holiday elegance to your Hanukkah table. The stenciled Menorah gives this table runner a unique and lovely look.

MATERIALS

Finished size: 11½" x 52"

White-on-white fabric – ⅔ yard
Three shades of blue fabric – ⅛ yard of each
Fourth blue fabric – ¼ yard
Backing – 1⅝ yards
Batting – 16" x 56" piece
Stencil brush
Paintbrush
Craft knife
Template plastic or Mylar
Fabric or craft paint – medium blue, navy blue, gold, yellow
Black fabric marker

Cutting

White-on-white
Cut two 8½" squares
  One 12" x 28" piece
First blue
Cut two 2" x 12" pieces
  One 1½" x 30" strip
Second blue
Cut one 1½" x 30" strip
Third blue
Cut eight 2" x 2½" pieces
Fourth blue
Cut ten 2½" x 3½" pieces
  Two 2½" x 4½" pieces
  Four 2¼" x 8½" pieces

Assembly

1. Sew together the 1½" x 30" strips of the first blue and second blue fabric. Cut the strip set into sixteen 1½" segments.

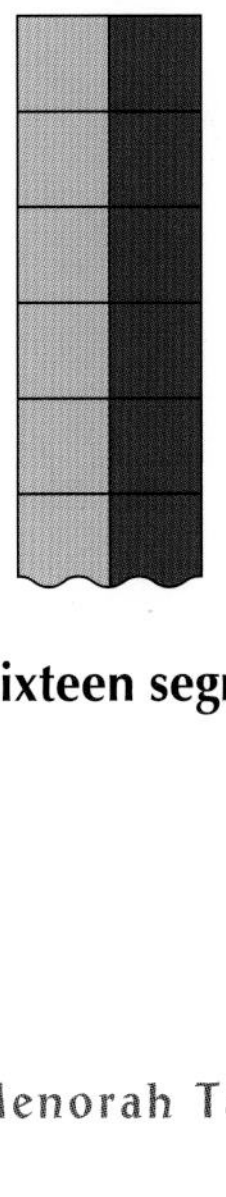

Cut sixteen segments

2. Sew two segments from step 1 together to make a Four-Patch block. Repeat to make eight blocks.

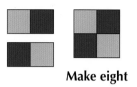

Make eight

3. Assemble the third blue and fourth blue pieces and the Four-Patch blocks into rows as shown to make two end border units. Sew together the rows and press.

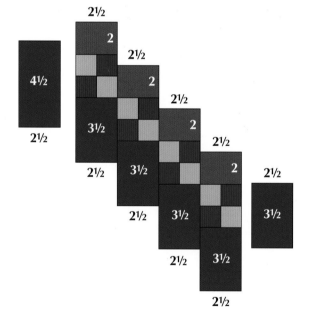

4. Using a rotary cutter and see-through ruler, trim the top and sides of the border units leaving a generous ¼" seam allowance beyond the corners of the Four-Patch block. Trim the bottom leaving a generous ½" seam allowance. It should measure 3" x 12".

5. Assemble the white-on-white squares, blue pieces, and patchwork border strips as shown to make two table runner end sections. Press.

6. Sew the 12" x 28" white-on-white piece between the two end sections. Press.

Finishing

1. Referring to "Stenciling" on page 9, cut stencils for the Menorah and halo from the patterns on page 62. Stencil to the table runner. Using a stencil brush, pounce on the glow from the candles.

2. With the black fabric marker, draw candlewicks and heat set the marker. Paint on the flames with gold paint.

3. Cut a 16" x 56" backing piece. With right sides together, layer the table runner top and backing onto the batting piece. Stitch ¼" from the table runner edge through all the layers, leaving a 6" opening on the side for turning. Trim the backing and batting even with the table runner top.

4. Trim the corners and turn right side out. Press and hand stitch the opening.

5. Machine quilt in the seam lines of the border sections and in the table runner center as desired.

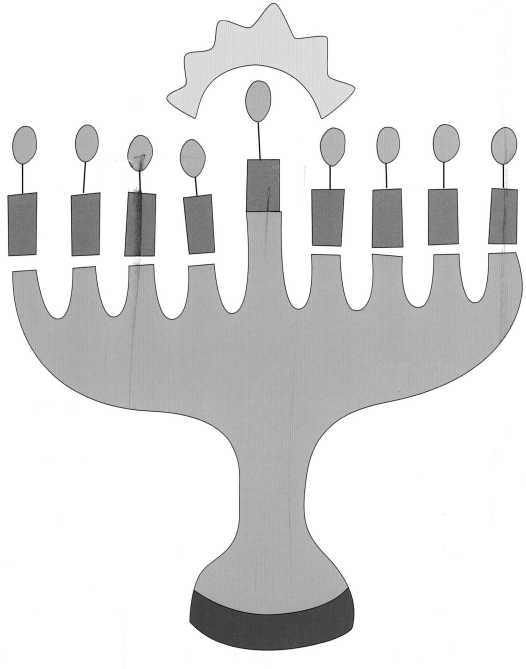

Stencil two

Happy Hanukkah

Welcome the season with this fun collection of happy Hanukkah houses that are paper pieced in this charming holiday quilt. You will add the delightful details with fusible appliqué, stamping, and marking pen.

MATERIALS

Finished size: 35" x 47¼"

Houses A and B fabric:
Roof – ¼ yard
Right side of house – ¼ yard
Left side of house and chimneys – ⅓ yard
Sky – ⅓ yard
Block borders – ¼ yard each of three
fabrics

Houses C and D fabric:
Roof – ¼ yard
Right side of house – ⅛ yard
Left side of house – ⅓ yard
Sky – ⅓ yard
Block borders – ¼ yard each of
three fabrics, 6" x 6" scrap for
corner squares
Star and window appliqués – ¼ yard
Octagon appliqués – ¼ yard
Sashing – ½ yard
Backing – 1½ yards
Binding – ½ yard
Batting – 40" x 52" piece
Fusible web – 1 yard

Template plastic or Mylar
Two art gum erasers
Craft knife
Paintbrush
Fabric markers – blue and black
Fabric or craft paint – light blue and
dark blue

Cutting

Blocks A and B
Top border
Cut two 2"-wide strips, then cut into
Twelve 6" pieces
Left border
Cut three 1¾"-wide strips, then cut into
Twelve 7½" pieces
Block B
Outside left border
Cut two 2"-wide strips , then cut into
Nine 7½" pieces

Blocks C and D
Bottom border
Cut two 1¾"-wide strips, then cut into
Twelve 6" pieces
Left border
Cut three 2"-wide strips, then cut into
Twelve 7¼" pieces
Block D
Top border
Cut two 2"-wide strips, then cut into
Nine 6" pieces

Corner Squares – Cut nine 2" squares

Sashing – Cut six 2¼" strips, then cut into

    Four 7½" pieces

    Four 14½" pieces

    Three 35½" strips

Binding – Five 2½" x 42" strips

Blocks

You will be paper piecing the block centers. and adding borders to create Blocks A, B, C, and D. The centers of Blocks A and B are paper pieced in the same fabrics and Blocks C and D are in the same fabrics.

Block A—Make three

1. Referring to "Paper Piecing" on page 88 and the piecing diagram below, piece the house centers for Block A. Piece each section in sequence, then sew together the sections. Use the sky fabric for pieces 2, 3, 6, and 8; the left

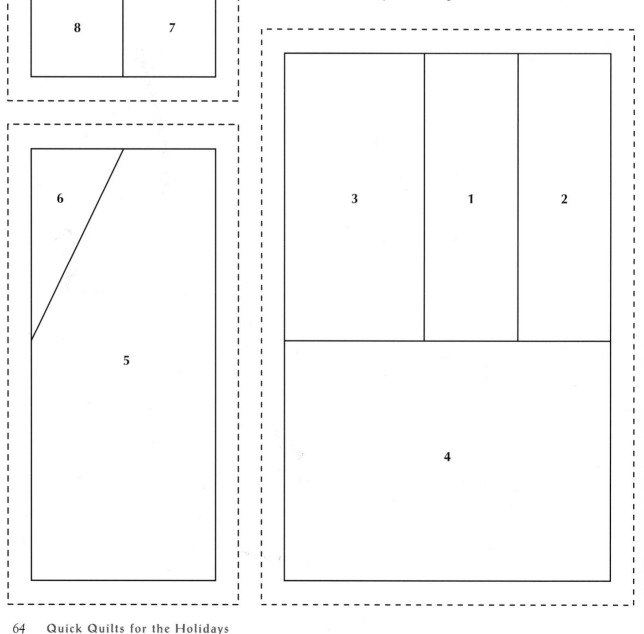

house fabric for pieces 1, 5, and 7; and the right house fabric for piece 4. Press. Trim block to a 6" square including the seam allowance.

2. Sew a 2" x 6" top border piece to the pieced house centers. Press. Add a 1¾" x 7½" left border piece to each. Press.

Block A

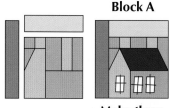

Make three

Block B—Make nine

1. Repeat steps 1 and 2 for Block A. To complete Block B, add a 2" x 7½" piece of sky fabric to the left side of each block. Press.

Block B

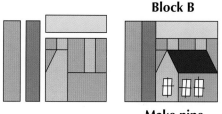

Make nine

Block C—Make three

1. Repeat step 1 for Block A to paper piece Block C house centers.

2. Sew a 1¾" x 6" bottom border piece and a 2" x 7¼" left border piece to the left sides of each block.

Block C

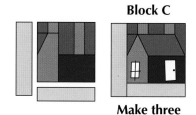

Make three

Block D—Make nine

1. Repeat steps 1 and 2 for Block C. To com-

plete Block D, sew nine 2" corner squares on the ends of nine 2" x 6" top border pieces. Press. Sew to the top of each block.

Block D

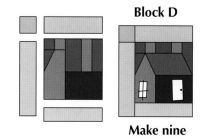

Make nine

Adding the Appliqué

1. From page 67, trace the roof, window, and door patterns onto template plastic and cut out. Referring to "Fusible Appliqué" on page 87, trace and cut twelve roofs from Blocks A and B roof fabric, twelve roofs from Blocks C and D roof fabric, forty-eight windows from white fabric, and twelve doors from Blocks A and B border fabric.

2. On the large side of an art gum eraser draw two parallel lines. With a craft knife, score and cut away the background to approximately ⅛". Refer to "Stamping" on page 8. With light blue paint, stamp lines on the twelve roof pieces for Blocks A and B. Let dry.

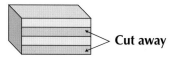

3. Repeat to make the stamp for the Blocks C and D roofs. Draw triangles as shown and cut away the background. With dark blue paint, stamp triangles on the twelve roof pieces for Blocks C and D.

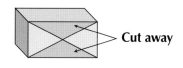

4. Fuse the roofs and three windows to Blocks A and B. Fuse roofs, one window, and a door to Blocks C and D.

5. With black fabric marker, draw windowpanes and doorknobs on each block. Heat set the marker. Machine satin stitch around the fused edges of the roofs.

Assembly

1. Sew together twenty-four blocks, four 2¼" x 7½" sashing pieces, four 2¼" x 14½" sashing pieces, and three 2¼" x 35½" sashing pieces as shown. Press between each step.

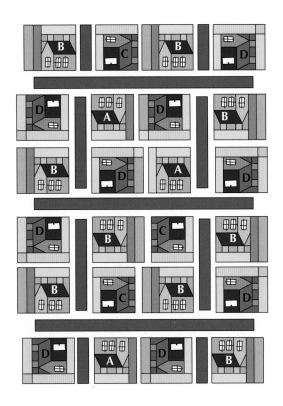

2. Trace the octagon and star patterns from page 67 onto template plastic and cut out. Trace six of each, fuse, and cut out of fabric.

3. Fuse stars to the center of the octagons and machine satin stitch around the edges of the stars. Stitch across the star points, and position the octagons with the star appliqués at the sashing intersections. Fuse and machine satin stitch the edges.

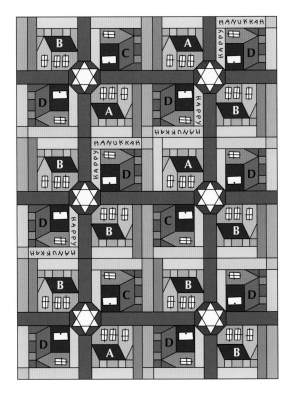

4. Referring to the lettering pattern on page 67, write "Happy Hanukkah" on four Block D's with the blue fabric marker as shown in the photo. Heat set the marker.

Finishing

1. Referring to "Layering and Quilting" on page 90, layer the top, batting, and backing together and baste. Quilt as desired.

2. Refer to "Binding" on page 90 and sew binding to the quilt.

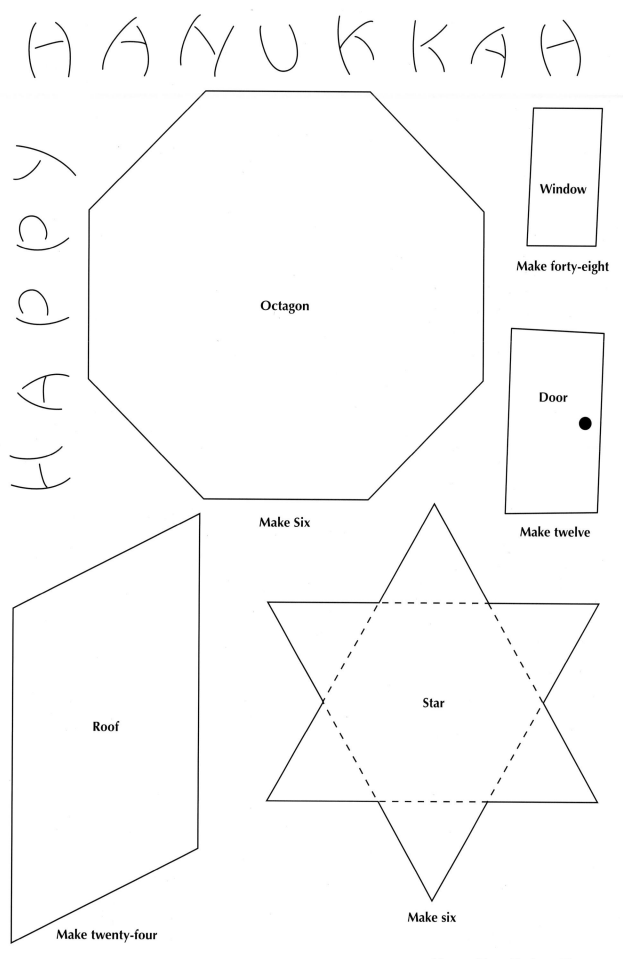

HAPPY HANUKKAH

Octagon

Make Six

Window

Make forty-eight

Door

Make twelve

Roof

Make twenty-four

Star

Make six

Merry Merry

And a merry, merry Christmas it will be when you make this fanciful quilt to add to your holiday décor. The festive paper-pieced tree is adorned with colorful painted ornaments that are fused and machine satin stitched.

MATERIALS

Finished size: 24" x 36"

White-on-white print fabric – 5/8 yard
Medium peach fabric – 1/4 yard
Light peach fabric – 1/4 yard
Cream print fabric – 1/3 yard
Red fabric – 1/8 yard
Light blue fabric – 1/8 yard
Dark blue, medium blue, browns, black
    fabric – scraps or small pieces
Dark green fabric – 1/3 yard
Medium green fabric – 1/3 yard
Red and green striped fabric – 3/8 yard
White fabric for appliqués – 3/8 yard
Backing – 7/8 yard
Batting – 28" x 40" piece
Facing – 1/3 yard
Fusible web – 1/2 yard
Black thread
Template plastic or Mylar
Air soluble marker
Black fabric marker
Fabric or craft paint—light blue, apple
    green, red, orange, lavender, yellow,
    mint green
Paintbrush

Cutting

White-on-white – Cut one 1" x 7¼" piece
    One 1¼" x 3¾" piece
    One 1¼" x 1¾" piece
    One 1¾" x 7" piece
    Three 2½" x 6" pieces
    Five 1¼" squares
Medium peach – Cut two 3¼" x 24½" pieces
Light peach – Cut two 1½" x 4" pieces
    One 4½" x 12¼" pieces
    One 5½" square
    One 5½" x 7¾" piece
    One 5½" x 10" piece
Cream print – Cut one 4½" x 5½" piece
    One 5" x 11½" piece
    One 5" x 10¾" piece
    One 5" x 16" piece
Red – Cut one 1¼" x 18" piece
Light blue – Cut three 2½" x 6" pieces
Dark blue – Cut two 1¼" x 1½" pieces
    Four 1¼" squares
Medium blue – Cut one 4¾" x 4½" piece
Browns – Cut one 1¾" square
    One 4" square
    One 2" x 6" piece
Facing – Cut four 2" x 42" strips

Assembly

1. Referring to "Paper Piecing" on page 88 and the piecing diagram below, paper piece the Christmas tree. Piece each section in sequence, then sew together the five sections.

Use dark green for pieces 1, 4, 8, and 13; medium green for pieces 7 and 10; and white-on-white print for pieces 2, 3, 5, 6, 9, 11, 12, 14, 15, 16, and 17.

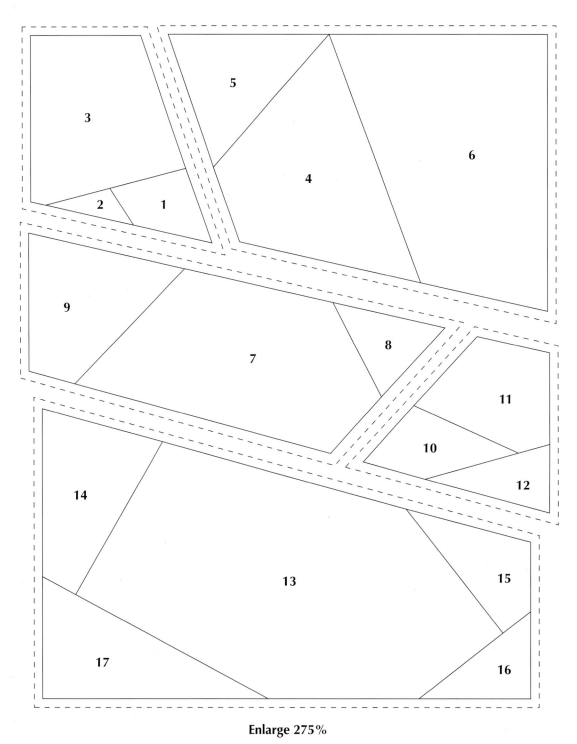

Enlarge 275%

2. Sew five 1¼" white-on-white squares and four 1¼" dark blue squares together in a strip. Press. Sew a 1" x 7¼" white-on-white piece to the top and press.

3. Sew the 1¾" brown square and the 1¾" x 7" white-on-white piece to the end of the unit from step 2. Press.

4. Referring to "Bias Strips" on page 89, fold the red and green striped fabric on the bias and cut a 1" x 4¾" strip. Sew it to the bottom of the 4½" x 4¾" medium blue piece. Press. Sew a 5" x 10¾" cream print piece to the side and press.

5. Sew the unit from step 3 to the bottom of the pieced Christmas tree. Sew the unit from step 4 to the top. Press.

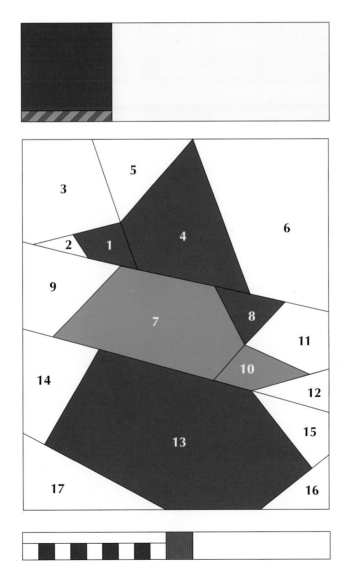

6. From the bias striped fabric from step 4, cut a 1" x 12¼" bias strip. Sew to the left side of a 4½" x 12¼" light peach piece. Press. Joining the short sides, sew a 5" x 11½" cream piece to the top and press.

7. From the bias striped fabric from step 4, cut a 1" x 16" bias strip. Sew to the right side of the 5" x 16" cream print piece. Press. Sew the 5½" x 7¾" light peach piece to the top and press.

8. Sew a 4" brown square between two 1½" x 4" light peach pieces. Add the 2" x 6" brown piece to the top and press.

9. Sew together the 5½" x 10" light peach piece, the unit from step 8, the 5½" light peach square, and the 4½" x 5½" cream print piece. Press.

10. Sew together in a strip two 1¼" x 1½" dark blue pieces, one 1¼" x 3¾" white-on-white piece, one 1¼" x 1¾" white-on-white piece, and one 1¼" x 18" red piece. Press.

11. Beginning with a white strip and alternating colors, sew together three 2½" x 6" white pieces and three 2½" x 6" light blue pieces. Press. Cut into two 2½" segments. Sew the segments together to make one 2½" x 24½" strip.

12. Sew together the Christmas tree center and the units from steps 6, 7, 9, 10, and 11. Add a 3¼" x 24½" medium peach piece to the top and bottom. Press.

Cut two segments

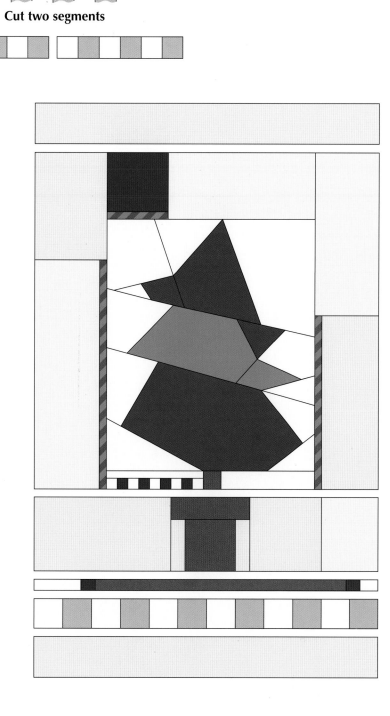

Finishing

1. Trace the ornament patterns on page 77 onto template plastic and cut out. With the air soluble marker, trace four round ornaments onto white fabric. Dilute the light blue and apple green paints with water to create a "watercolor" effect. Experiment with a scrap of fabric to get the desired effect, then paint the ornaments. Let dry.

2. Repeat step 1 to trace and paint four small stars with diluted yellow paint. Trace four large star ornaments and paint with diluted red, lavender, yellow, and mint green paints. Trace and paint four heart ornaments with diluted red paint and four vertical ornaments with diluted orange, red, and apple green paints. Let dry.

3. With the black fabric marker, draw the outlines and details on the ornaments.

4. Referring to "Fusible Appliqué" on page 87, iron fusible web to the wrong side of the ornaments, trim, and fuse to the wallhanging. Machine satin stitch around the ornaments with black thread.

5. Trace the reversed "Merry" pattern from page 76 onto template plastic and cut out. Trace it three times onto fusible web and fuse to black fabric. Cut out and fuse to the wallhanging. Machine satin stitch around the edges with black thread.

6. Referring to "Layering and Quilting" on page 90, layer the wallhanging top, batting, and backing and baste. Quilt as desired.

7. Refer to "Facings" on page 91 to add facings to the back of the wallhanging.

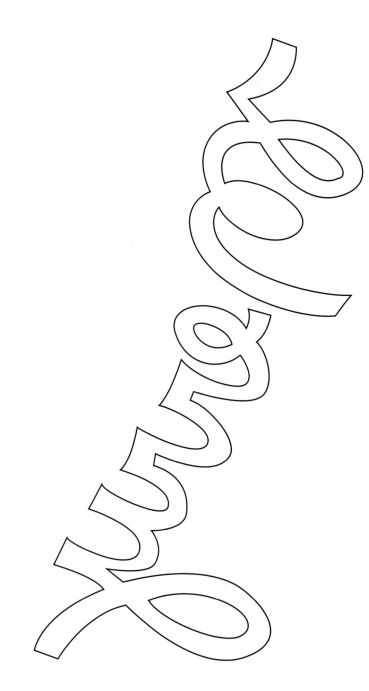

Trace three

Trace four

Trace four

Trace four

Trace four

Trace four

Christmas Doves

These charming Christmas doves echo the peace and joy of the holiday season. Add their unique touch to your own home by creating this festive quilt with hand appliqué and stenciling.

MATERIALS

Finished size: 52" x 58"

Tan fabric – 2⅓ yards
Dark green fabric – ⅓ yard
Medium green fabric – ¼ yard
Turquoise fabric – ½ yard
Gold fabric – ¼ yard
Red fabric – ⅔ yard
Light green fabric for appliqué
    vines – 1 yard
Backing – 3¼ yards
Binding – ¾ yard
Batting – 56" x 62" piece
Bias press bars – ½"
Craft knife
Template plastic or Mylar
Stencil brush
Fabric or craft paint – light blue,
    medium blue, dark gray, tan, rust,
    and medium taupe

Cutting

Tan

Cut five 6½" x 54½" strips lengthwise from fabric

Cut nine 1¼"-wide strips, then cut three into Eighty 1¼" squares

Cut five 1½"-wide strips, then cut into Forty-four 4¼" pieces

Cut three 2"-wide strips

Dark green

Cut three 1¼"-wide strips

Cut three 2"-wide strips

Medium green

Cut two 2"-wide strips, then cut into Forty 2" squares

Turquoise – Cut fifteen 1"-wide strips

Gold – Cut three 2"-wide strips

Red – Cut six 3½"-wide strips

Binding – Cut six 2½"-wide strips

Assembly

1. Refer to "Bias Strips" on page 89 and cut enough 1½" light green bias strips to piece together and make five strips, each 60" long.

2. Follow the manufacturer's instructions on the press bars to make five bias tubes for the vines.

3. Position the bias vines in a scalloped pattern on five 6½" x 52½" tan strips. Refer to the color photo for placement of the vines.

4. Cut five 1"-wide turquoise strips in half and sew half to the end of the remaining ten turquoise strips. Trim each to 52½" and sew them to the sides of the appliquéd strips. Press.

5. Sew three 1¼"-wide dark green strips and three 1¼"-wide tan strips together in pairs to make three strip sets. Press. Cut into eighty 1¼" segments.

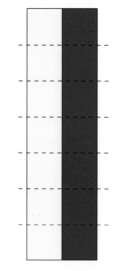

Make three strip sets

6. Sew a 1¼" tan square to each segment from step 5. Press.

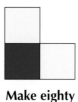

Make eighty

7. Sew forty 2" medium green squares between eighty units from step 6. Press.

Make forty

8. Sew three 1¼"-wide tan strips, three 2"-wide dark green strips, and three 2"-wide tan strips together to make three strip sets. Press and cut into eighty 1¼" segments.

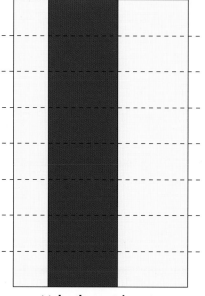

Make three strip sets

9. Referring to the diagram, sew a unit from step 8 to each side of a unit from step 7, making forty units. Press.

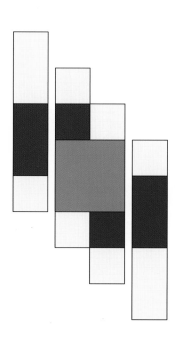

10. Using a clear acrylic ruler and a rotary cutter, trim each segment as shown, using a generous ¼" seam allowance beyond the outer seam intersection.

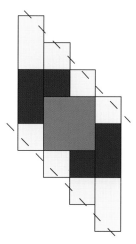

11. For each of the four pieced strips, alternate eleven tan 1½" x 4¼" strips and ten diamond units from step 10, beginning and ending with a tan strip. Trim the tan strips even with the pieced diamond units.

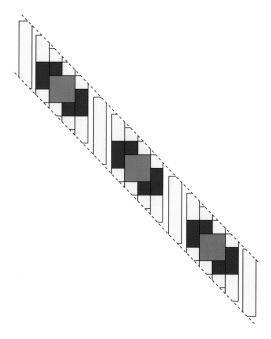

12. Sew together the strips from steps 4 and 11 as shown.

13. Cut one 2" gold strip in half and sew one half to each of the two remaining gold strips. Trim to 52½" and add to the sides of the quilt. Repeat to add 3½" red borders to the sides and to the top and bottom.

Finishing

1. Refer to "Stenciling" on page 9. From template plastic, cut stencils for the wing, body, and legs. Using light blue, medium blue, and dark gray paint, stencil five birds onto each appliqué vine, referring to the color photo for placement.

2. Carefully clean the paint from the bird stencil. Reverse and add birds to the opposite side of the vines using tan, rust, and medium taupe paint.

3. Referring to "Layering and Quilting" on page 90, layer the top, batting, and backing together and baste. Quilt as desired.

4. Refer to "Binding" on page 90 and sew binding to the quilt.

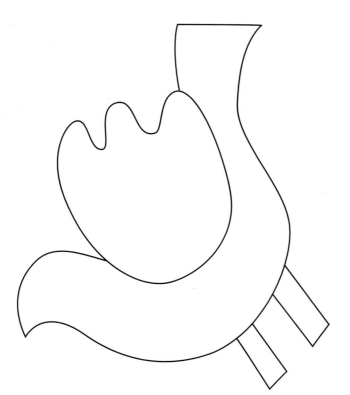

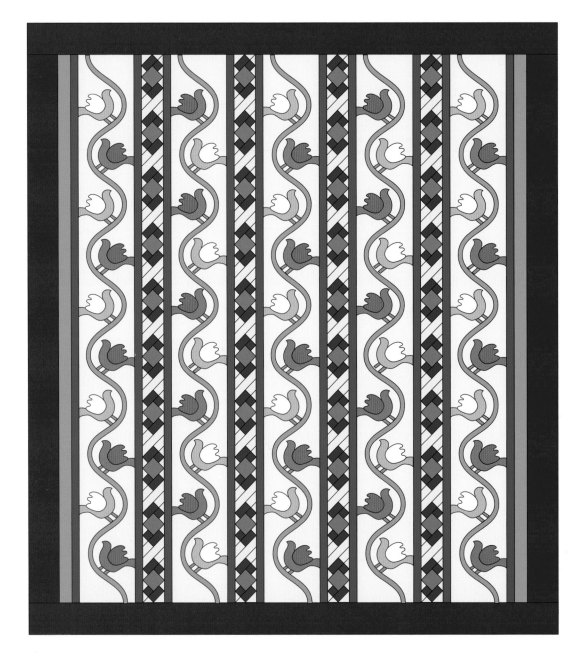

Quilting
Techniques

In addition to the specialty techniques that you will use to complete your book projects, I have included a few tips and techniques to help you complete the construction and finishing of them as well.

Before you begin, here are a few basic tips to keep in mind—

- Fabric requirements are based on a 42"-width, and strips usually cut on the crossgrain of the fabric with the selvages together.
- Use a ¼" seam allowance for all projects unless otherwise indicated.
- Press between each step, and generally press toward the darker fabric.
- Read all directions before beginning the project.

HAND APPLIQUÉ

Hand appliqué is a favorite traditional technique for adding decorative details to larger areas on a quilt. There are a number of different appliqué techniques that can be used, but for the projects in this book I have used the freezer-paper technique. You may substitute your own favorite method of appliqué if you prefer.

Begin by selecting a cotton thread that matches the appliqué pieces as closely as possible. You will also need a long, thin needle for stitching and pins for holding the shapes until they are sewn.

Freezer-Paper Appliqué

Trace the appliqué shapes onto template plastic and cut them out. Then with the shiny side up, trace around the template onto freezer paper and cut out. Pin the freezer-paper shape onto the wrong side of the fabric and cut out leaving a turn-under allowance of ³⁄₁₆"–¼" extending beyond the freezer paper.

Press the seam allowance to the shiny side of freezer paper, turning the edge with a hot iron as you go around the freezer-paper template.

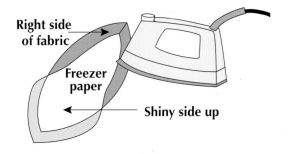

Position the appliqué shape onto the background and secure with a pin. Entering from the wrong side of the appliqué shape, bring the needle up through the fabric on the folded edge. Using a blind stitch, stitch along the folded edge to join the appliqué shape to the background.

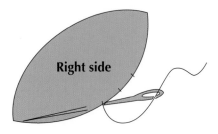

To remove the freezer paper, make a slit in the background fabric behind the appliqué, which is ¼" from the stitching line. Loosen the paper with a tweezers and pull out.

FUSIBLE APPLIQUÉ

Fusible appliqué is a quick and easy way of adding appliqué accents to your quilts without turning under the edges or hand sewing. Fusible web is used to adhere the appliqué shapes to the background with an iron. A number of excellent fusible webs are on the market and available at your local quilt shop. Follow the manufacturer's instructions for adding appliqués to your quilt using their product.

Once the fusible appliqués have been added, I recommend finishing the edges with machine stitching.

MITERED BORDERS

To add mitered borders to your quilt, begin by measuring the length of the quilt top and adding two times the width of the border, plus 5". This is the length you need to cut or piece for the side borders. Using pins, mark the measured quilt top length on the border strips. Match the center and measured length to the quilt top.

1. Place pins at the centers of all four sides of the quilt top and both side borders. Pin, matching center pins, and stitch the strips to the sides of the quilt top. Stop and backstitch at the seam allowance line, ¼" from the

edge. The excess length will extend beyond each edge. Press seams towards the border.

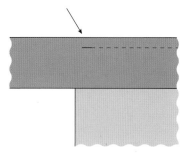

2. Determine the length needed for the top and bottom borders the same way, measuring the width of the quilt top through the center including each side border. Mark and pin the measured width on the borders. Match to quilt top. Again, pin, stitch up to the ¼" seam line, and backstitch. The border strips extend beyond each end. To create the miter, lay the corner on the ironing board. Working with the quilt right side up, lay one strip on top of the adjacent border.

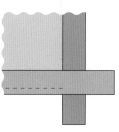

3. Fold the top border strip under itself so that it meets the edge of the outer border and forms a 45° angle. Press and pin the fold in place.

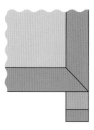

4. Position a 90° triangle or ruler at the corner to check that the border is flat and square. When everything is in place, press the fold firmly.

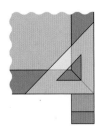

5. Fold the center section of the top diagonally from the corner, right sides together, and align the long edges of the border strips. On the wrong side, place pins near the pressed fold in the corner to secure the border strips.

6. Beginning at the inside corner, backstitch and stitch along the fold toward the outside point, being careful not to allow any stretching to occur. Backstitch at the end. Trim the excess border fabric to a ¼" seam allowance. Press the seam open.

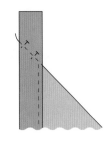

PAPER PIECING

Paper piecing is an easy way to sew accurate blocks with small or irregularly shaped pieces. Sew on the side of the paper with the printed lines and place the fabric on the nonprinted side. Use a smaller than usual stitch length (#1.5–1.8 or 18–20 stitches per inch) and a slightly larger needle (size 90/14). This makes the paper removal easier, and the smaller stitches can't be pulled apart when you tear off the paper.

With paper piecing you don't need to worry about the grain of the fabric so you can cut your pieces from small scraps of fabric. You will be stitching on paper and that stabilizes the block.

Trace or photocopy the number of paper-piecing patterns need for your project. Then cut the fabric pieces slightly larger than necessary—about ¾" larger. They do not need to be perfect shapes, which is one of the joys of paper piecing!

Follow the number sequence when piecing. If your paper-piecing pattern is divided into sections, piece each section separately according to the number sequence and then sew the sections together.

1. Begin by pinning piece #1 in place on the blank side of the paper, but make sure you don't place the pin anywhere near a seam line. Hold the paper up to the light to make sure the piece covers the area it is supposed to cover with the seam allowance also generously covered.

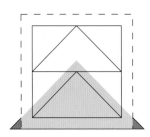

2. Fold the pattern back at the stitching line and trim the fabric to a ¼" seam allowance.

3. Cut piece #2 large enough to cover the area of #2 on the paper, plus a generous seam allowance. It's a good idea to cut each piece larger than you think necessary. It might seem a bit wasteful, but it's easier than ripping out tiny stitches! Align the edge with the trimmed seam allowance of piece #1, right sides together, and pin. Paper side up, stitch on line.

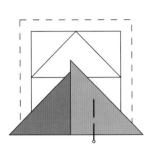

4. Continue stitching each piece in order, being sure to fold back the paper pattern and trim the seam allowance to ¼" before adding the next piece.

5. Trim around the finished unit to the ¼" seam allowance. Leave the paper intact until after the sections of the block have been sewn together and the finished blocks are sewn together, then carefully remove it.

BIAS STRIPS

Bias strips are cut on the diagonal line of the fabric which gives the fabric a different look than cutting on the straight grain. They are also used in bindings or appliqué to go around curves without wrinkling or puckering.

1. Fold down the corner of a straight piece of fabric, forming a triangle. Cut on this folded line which will be the bias of the fabric.

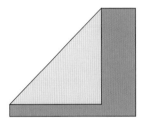

2. Using a see-through ruler and rotary cutter, measure from the bias edge and cut strips the width needed.

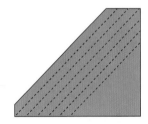

LAYERING AND QUILTING

1. Spread the backing wrong side up and tape the edges down with masking tape. If you are working on a carpet you can use T-pins to secure the backing to the carpet. Center the batting on top, smoothing out any folds. Place the quilt top right side up on top of the batting and backing, making sure it's centered.

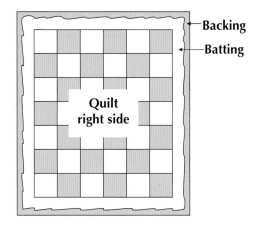

2. Baste the quilt layers together with safety pins placed a minimum of 3"–4" apart, beginning in the center and moving towards the edges. If you prefer, baste the layers together with thread using a long needle and light-colored thread.

3. Quilting, whether by hand or machine, enhances the design of the quilt. You may choose to quilt-in-the-ditch, echo quilt, use patterns from design books or stencils, or do free-motion quilting.

BINDING

Trim excess batting and backing from the quilt. Piece together the binding strips using a diagonal seam to make a continuous binding strip. Press the seams open, then press the entire strip in half lengthwise with wrong sides together.

With raw edges even, pin the binding to the edge of the quilt a few inches away from the corner, and leave the first few inches of the binding unattached. Start sewing using a ¼" seam allowance.

Stop ¼" away from the first corner, backstitch one stitch, and pivot the quilt with the needle down into the quilt.

Lift the needle and fold the binding at a right angle so it extends straight above the quilt.

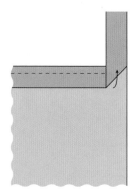

Then bring the binding strip down even with the edge of the quilt.

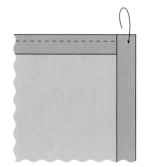

Begin sewing at the folded edge and continue in this manner until the binding is sewn to the quilt top. Fold binding to the quilt back and hand stitch.

FACING

To face the side edges of a quilt, cut strips 2" or 3"-wide and the same lengths you would use for binding. With right sides together and raw edges matching, pin each side strip to the quilt top and sew with a 1/4" seam.

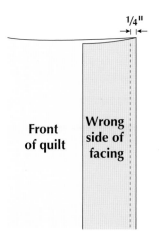

From the front of the quilt, press the strip away from the seam line. Topstitch 1/8" from the seam through all layers.

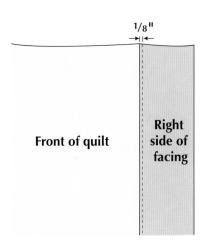

Turn the quilt over and fold the facing onto the back of the quilt, making sure a tiny edge of the quilt top rolls to the back. Turn raw edges under and hem to the back of quilt.

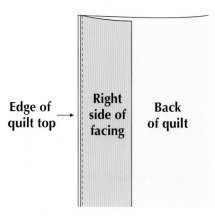

Cut the facing for the bottom edge 1" longer than the quilt width to allow for a finished corner. Sew the facing right sides together with the front bottom edge, making sure the strip extends 1/2" beyond the quilt at each end.

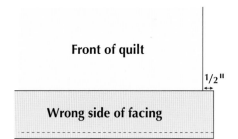

Topstitch, fold back, press, and hand stitch to the back, folding in the excess at each end.

EMBROIDERY STITCHES

Satin Stitch

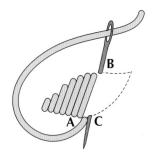

Stem Stitch

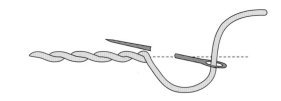

Blanket Stitch

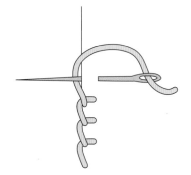

Index

Bibliography

Here are some of my favorite quilting and embellishing books. Some are great for learning technique while others I love just for inspiration!

ANDERSON, ALEX
Start Quilting with Alex Anderson: Six Projects for First-time Quilters
Lafayette, CA: C&T Publishing, 1997

BAHOUTH, CANDACE
Medieval Needlepoint
London, England: Conran Octopus, 1994

BROMMER, GERALD
Collage Techniques, A Guide for Artists and Illustrators
New York, NY: Watson Guptil, 1994

HARGRAVE, HARRIET
Heirloom Machine Quilting: A Comprehensive Guide to Hand Quilted Effects Using Your Sewing Machine, 3rd Edition.
Lafayette, CA: C & T Publishing, 1995

McCAFFERY, CANDACE
A Show of Hands
New York, NY: Hearst Books, 1994

MATTHEWS, KATE
Molas
Asheville, NC: Lark Books, 1998

NADELSTERN, PAULA
Kaleidoscopes & Quilts
Lafayette, CA: C&T Publishing, 1996

SIENKIEWICZ, ELLY
Appliqué 12 Easy Ways! Charming Quilts, Giftable Projects, & Timeless Techniques
Lafayette, CA: C&T Publishing, 1993

About the Author

Trice Boerens is a freelance designer with experience in designing a wide mix of creative products. Everything from needlework books to rubber stamps and greeting cards to furniture . . . she's worked in all them. Even designing tattoos!

She has designed for such companies as *Better Homes and Gardens*, Coats & Clark, and the Disney Corporation, to name a few. Always looking for a new creative challenge, she has also worked as a product development consultant, an illustrator, and a photo stylist. Her latest venture, *Quick Quilts for the Holidays*, combines her wide range of creative talents and experience.

A graduate of Brigham Young University in art education, today Trice makes her home in Ogden, Utah, with her husband and four children.

Other Fine Books from C&T Publishing

250 Continuous-Line Quilting Designs for Hand, Machine & Long-Arm Quilters, Laura Lee Fritz

Art of Classic Quiltmaking, The, Harriet Hargrave & Sharyn Craig

Art of Machine Piecing, The: How to Achieve Quality Workmanship Through a Colorful Journey, Sally Collins

Bouquet of Quilts, A: Garden-Inspired Projects for the Home, Edited by Jennifer Rounds & Cyndy Lyle Rymer

Butterflies & Blooms: Designs for Appliqué & Quilting, Carol Armstrong

Come Listen to My Quilts: • Playful Projects • Mix & Match Designs, Kristina Becker

Create Your Own Quilt Labels!, Kim Churbuck

Enchanted Views: Quilts Inspired by Wrought-Iron Designs, Dilys Fronks

Fabric Stamping Handbook, The: • Fun Projects • Tips & Tricks • Unlimited Possibilities, Jean Ray Laury

Free Stuff for Quilters on the Internet, 3rd Edition, Judy Heim & Gloria Hansen

Garden-Inspired Quilts: Design Journals for 12 Quilt Projects, Jean Wells & Valori Wells

Kaleidoscope Artistry, Cozy Baker

Kids Start Quilting with Alex Anderson: • 7 Fun & Easy Projects • Quilts for Kids by Kids • Tips for Quilting with Children, Alex Anderson

Laurel Burch Quilts: Kindred Creatures, Laurel Burch

Lone Star Quilts and Beyond: Step-by-Step Projects and Inspiration, Jan Krentz

Machine Embroidery and More: Ten Step-by-Step Projects Using Border Fabrics & Beads, Kristen Dibbs

Mastering Machine Appliqué, 2nd Edition: The Complete Guide Including: • Invisible Machine Appliqué • Satin Stitch • Blanket Stitch & Much More, Harriet Hargrave

Paper Piecing Picnic: Fun-Filled Projects for Every Quilter, From the Editors and Contributors of Quilter's Newsletter Magazine and Quiltmaker Magazine

Paper Piecing with Alex Anderson: • Tips • Techniques • 6 Projects, Alex Anderson

Photo Transfer Handbook, The: Snap It, Print It, Stitch It!, Jean Ray Laury

Pieced Vegetables, Ruth B. McDowell

Provence Quilts and Cuisine, Marie-Christine Flocard & Cosabeth Parriaud

Quilting Back to Front: Fun & Easy No-Mark Techniques, Larraine Scouler

Quilting with Carol Armstrong: • 30 Quilting Patterns • Appliqué Designs • 16 Projects, Carol Armstrong

Show Me How to Machine Quilt: A Fun, No-Mark Approach, Kathy Sandbach

Strips 'n Curves: A New Spin on Strip Piecing, Louisa L. Smith

FOR MORE INFORMATION WRITE FOR A FREE CATALOG:

C&T Publishing, Inc.
P.O. Box 1456
Lafayette, CA 94549
(800) 284-1114
e-mail: ctinfo@ctpub.com
website: www.ctpub.com

FOR QUILTING SUPPLIES:

Cotton Patch Mail Order
3405 Hall Lane, Dept. CTB
Lafayette, CA 94549
(800) 835-4418
(925) 283-7883
e-mail:quiltusa@yahoo.com
website: www.quiltusa.com

Note: Fabrics used in the quilts shown may not be currently available since fabric manufacturers keep most fabrics in print for only a short time.